The website moan... Sue Hedges and Ang... about their men ove... ...aunch in 2007 it has become v...y popular with women all over the world, attracting considerable attention with its lively forum, community site and chat room designed for girly conversation.

Juliana Foster is a former publisher and the author of the bestselling *The Girls' Book: How to be the Best at Everything*. She lives with her husband in Kent.

Moan about Men

A joyful guide to the things men do
that drive women mad

Juliana Foster

moanabout
'men'

headline

First published in 2008
by HEADLINE PUBLISHING GROUP

First published in paperback in 2009
by HEADLINE PUBLISHING GROUP

1

Cataloguing in Publication Data is available from the British Library

Illustrations by Joy Gosney

Design by Viv Mullett

Paperback ISBN 978 0 7553 1842 1

Typeset in Cheltenham Light ITC by The Flying Fish Studios Ltd

Printed and bound in Great Britain by
CPI Mackays, Chatham ME5 8TD

Headline's policy is to use papers that are natural, renewable and recyclable
products and made from wood grown in sustainable forests. The logging and
manufacturing processes are expected to conform to the environmental
regulations of the country of origin.

HEADLINE PUBLISHING GROUP
An Hachette Livre UK Company
338 Euston Road
London NW1 3BH

www.headline.co.uk
www.hachettelivre.co.uk

Contents

Introduction   vii

The Great Outdoors   1

Family Man   23

Boys and Their Toys   65

Bad Habits   99

Looking Good, Feeling Good   125

Men in Love   143

Uniquely Male   177

Introduction

Men. We love them, we hate them, they drive us mad, we couldn't do without them. They can be reckless, thoughtless, lazy, impractical, irritating, tedious, rude, bossy, grumpy, arrogant, confusing, obnoxious, tricky, outrageous, repulsive and downright weird. Yet at the same time they can be amusing, charming, loving, gentle, kind, helpful, thoughtful and generally wonderful. It's no wonder, then, that we women sometimes feel so confused and conflicted about the men in our lives that we don't know whether we are coming or going. The one thing we do know, however, is that, no matter how irritating they can sometimes be, no matter how much frustration and heartache they sometimes cause us, life would be terribly dull without them.

We can try to teach our men to be more considerate, more tidy, more helpful – in short, more like women. Sometimes we even succeed in some small way – the dishes are washed, an anniversary is remembered, a football match is missed in favour of a day out with the family – but deep down we know we can't fundamentally change them, and, let's face it, we probably wouldn't want to.

Thank goodness, then, for our female friends. Thank goodness for girls' nights in or out with copious amounts of wine, chick flicks, enormous bars of chocolate and sympathetic shoulders to cry on. Thank goodness for our ability to laugh with each other about the things that drive us bonkers about the men in our lives. Thank goodness for all these things because, as we all know, there's nothing quite like a jolly good moan about men!

The Great Outdoors

Barbecues

These days, it is not uncommon for men to enjoy conducting the odd culinary experiment in the kitchen (although sometimes we wish they wouldn't; see Cooking), but it is fair to say that, on the whole, the preparation and serving of food is usually left to the womenfolk. Come the summer months, however, as soon as the sun wearily battles its way through the clouds, gardens the length and breadth of the country are filled with the sounds of men joyfully preparing for one of the Great British summer rituals: the barbecue. They love this yearly ritual and will not easily be deterred from performing it.

It is easy to deduce what appeals so much to men about barbecues. They involve: a) enormous slabs of meat, b) fire and c) copious amounts of beer. Not to mention the chance to wear an amusing apron that makes him look like either a bodybuilder or a scantily clad woman, or one bearing a hilarious slogan, such as 'Licensed to grill'.

Another reason why men love to grill outdoors is all the paraphernalia that come with it, such as giant utensils and various flammable, highly dangerous chemicals. And the barbecue itself, of course. In men's minds, when it comes to barbecues, size really does matter. You can get barbecues so enormous that they will take up the entire garden, leaving only a tiny square foot of grass free to accommodate your guests, who will

4

have to huddle together to avoid the ten-foot-high flames. The world's most expensive barbecue – made, of course, Down Under – costs a cool £20,000. In actual fact, it is not a barbecue at all. Oh no, it is an 'outdoor kitchen centre' and comes equipped with such necessities as a fridge, electric wine cooler and sink. With a price tag like that, you would expect it to breed, rear, slaughter and prepare a herd of rare-breed cattle for your eating pleasure.

One of the most irritating things about men and barbecues is that they expect you to be grateful that you have been 'given a break from doing the cooking', even though, of course, all they have done is burnt a few pieces of meat. All the preparation and the clearing up afterwards is left to the women, as the men, exhausted after their hard day's labour, settle down on the sofa for a nice beer-soaked snooze.

∽∽∽∽∽∽∽∽∽∽∽∽∽∽∽∽∽∽∽∽∽

A Typical Great British Barbecue

9 a.m. Man stands at window, anxiously looking for any rogue rain clouds that could ruin his moment of glory.

9.30 a.m. Man decides it is safe to go ahead

and wanders into garage to retrieve barbecue.
Woman drives to supermarket with shopping list
to buy food.

10.30 a.m. Woman returns. No sign of man to
help bring in shopping. No sign of barbecue. Man
still in garage, tinkering with half-built ham radio/
reorganising toolbox/pointlessly hammering nails
into wall.

11.00 a.m. Woman finishes putting away
shopping and gets to work chopping vegetables,
making salad dressing, preparing dessert,
marinating meat, unloading dishwasher and
gathering together the necessary glasses, plates
and cutlery. Man finally emerges from garage with
barbecue, which has not been cleaned out since
last outing, and dumps ash on lawn. No need to
clear it up, as 'the wind will blow it away'.

11.30 a.m. Barbecue is lit. Leaping wall of flames.
Woman calls fire brigade to warn them to be on
standby. Man satisfied with morning's work and has
first beer of the day.

12.00 p.m. Guests begin to arrive. Women gather
in kitchen to help with preparations. Men stand
around barbecue with beer.

12.30 p.m. Women bring out plates of meat.

Man puts meat on barbecue.

1.30 p.m. Meat suitably burnt. Man's work is done. Cue much back-slapping. Time to eat. More beer.

2.30 p.m. Women begin clearing-up proceedings. Men watch the footie.

Accidents

It is an incontrovertible fact that men are more accident-prone than women. Accident statistics show that adult males are three times as likely to die from injuries as women, and two to five times as likely to be admitted to hospital as a result of injury. This is not, say the experts, because men are clumsier than women, but because men are more likely to indulge in 'risky behaviour' – in other words, stupid behaviour.

From infancy onwards, men love to mess around with things that are likely to maim, burn, bite, cripple, decapitate or in other ways injure them. They scoff at basic health and safety practices and any suggestion that perhaps the best place to mend the still-plugged-in radio is not while sitting on the edge of a full bathtub is treated as a most heinous insult to their manhood.

It is no wonder then that they are always coming up with new and interesting ways to hurt themselves. In the interests of research (and in the interests of having a jolly good laugh at someone else's expense), let's take a look at some extreme examples of male idiocy that made headlines across the world.

❧❧❧❧❧❧❧❧❧❧❧❧❧❧❧❧❧❧❧❧❧❧❧

- ❖ A student from Exeter was making bread when the mixer clogged and came to a halt. Without turning the machine off first, he started pulling out bits of dough, until eventually it unclogged, whirled into action and broke his arm in four places. Ouch. A painful lesson learned, right? Well, no. A few weeks later he was describing his accident to some friends and decided to give them a demonstration. In went his hand and, yes, you've guessed it, he broke his arm once again.

- ❖ In 1983, an American man decided to fulfil a lifelong dream to fly. He purchased 45 weather balloons and a few tanks of helium and set his plans in motion. The idea was to attach the balloons to a patio chair, which was in turn anchored with a thick rope to his car. At his signal, his accomplices would cut the rope, whereupon he would float up to about 100 feet above his backyard, enjoy the view for a while and then pop the balloons one by one with a pellet gun until he came safely back down again. Unfortunately, things didn't quite go to plan. Having secured himself snugly in his chair, along with the pellet gun and some beer and sandwiches, Lawnchair Larry, as he became known, gave the signal for take-off. Up he floated. And then up and up and up and up some more, until he was a good three miles above the ground. At this point, he realised that popping the balloons was perhaps not a very good idea, so on he floated for nearly an hour (thank goodness for those sandwiches!), until he eventually got tangled up in some power lines and was able to clamber back down to the ground. He was immediately arrested and when asked why he had attempted to pull off such a monumentally stupid stunt, he simply replied, 'Well, a man can't just sit around.' Nice one, Larry!

❖ A 22-year-old man from Tennessee was at a friend's barbecue when, horrors of horrors, they

realised they were running low on charcoal.
'No problem,' said the helpful young chap, 'I'll
pop out and get some.' But there *was* a problem
because, bafflingly, he then proceeded to load
the smouldering barbecue onto the back of his
pickup truck and took it off with him. Not the
most advisable course of action under any
circumstances, but particularly not when you
also have a tank of propane in the back of your
vehicle. The ensuing fireball was luckily put out
in time to rescue the man, but presumably the
barbecue perished.

❖ A man had his lip bitten off when he attempted
to kiss a nurse shark while diving off the coast of
Florida. He later told reporters he had kissed many
sharks in his time and that the reason things had
gone awry this time was because the shark in
question had been upside down. So here is a
lesson for us all: only attempt to snog a shark
when it is the right way up.

❖ A young Bristol man was bored of bog-standard,
run-of-the-mill bungee-jumping and decided to
step things up a notch by setting himself on fire

while bungee-jumping (illegally) off the Clifton Suspension Bridge, whereupon he would cut the rope and plunge into the water, thus extinguishing the flames. Sadly, the knife he carried with him was not sharp enough to slice through the rope immediately, so he dangled there, flames leaping around him, for a good 30 seconds before he succeeded. As he lay in the burns unit of the local hospital a spokesperson (spokesperson? Surely a spokes*man*) for the Dangerous Sports Club told the BBC, unbelievably, 'His heart was in the right place.'

❖ In 1999, Gordon Lyons from Darwin, Australia made headlines when he survived being bitten not once, but nine times by a king brown snake, one of the deadliest creatures in the world. He was driving along with a pal when they spotted the snake at the side of the road. Thinking that it would be an excellent prize to show off to their mates down the pub, the two men pulled over and got out of the car. Gordon, who admitted to having been drunk at the time, explained that his fatal mistake was picking up the snake with his left hand, because he was holding a beer in his right.

He failed to get a
proper grip on
the snake,
which
promptly bit
him on the
hand. Having
wrestled with the
snake for a while,
he managed to pull
it off, stuffed it into
a plastic bag and
threw it into the back
of the car. What
happened next truly does beggar belief. As Gordon
explained to gobsmacked reporters, 'For some
stupid reason, I stuck my hand back in the bag, and
it must have smelled blood, and it bit me another
eight times.' By now, unsurprisingly, Gordon was
feeling rather woozy – 'My mate was trying to keep
me awake by whacking me on the head and
pouring beer on me' – and it is a miracle that he
survived the attack, albeit with extensive injuries.

Sheds

What is the deal with men and their sheds? The special place sheds have in men's hearts is a centuries-old phenomenon: the shed (or '*scead*', meaning 'partial darkness') is thought to have originated in the Dark Ages. It is also a universal phenomenon, at least in the Western world: it's not just British men who like to potter around in wooden boxes with roofs. In Australia, for example, the Men's Shed Movement is booming, and groups of men cram themselves into sheds all over the country to hammer nails into things and talk about their feelings. It's nice that these men are talking about their feelings – being Australian, it is clearly something of a breakthrough – but why must they do it in sheds? It's baffling.

Shed enthusiasts, or 'sheddists' (yes, there is an actual word for them) are passionate to the point of obsession. There are websites devoted solely to pictures of different garden sheds, like porn for sheddists, including one called, appropriately enough, 'Readers' Sheds'. A man called Gordon Thorburn wrote an entire book about them, which tells the stories of 40 proud shed-owners and their sheds, each of which 'is accompanied by photographs of the inner sanctum and of the customized exterior', according to Amazon.

Ernest Hemingway, Roald Dahl, Dylan Thomas and George Bernard Shaw were all sheddists, so it is clear that the humble shed can be an inspirational setting to creative types. But the average male probably isn't knocking up a literary masterpiece during the many hours he spends in there; so what exactly is he doing?

The simple answer is: not a lot. The shed is a refuge for men. More specifically, it is a refuge away from women. Sheds are not women-friendly environments. They tend to be cramped, grubby, dilapidated and full of spiders. Why on earth would we want to sit in them for hours on end? We prefer our outside structures to be more aesthetically pleasing and luxurious. Men know this and they use it to their advantage.

The shed is a place for him to keep all the junk he's been hoarding for years, the stuff he knows you'd throw in a skip in the blink of an eye given half the chance. Thus his piles of tattered *Beano* comics, his football memorabilia, his ancient stamp albums and the model aeroplanes he painstakingly put together when he was a child are kept in a safe, albeit damp, environment, well away from you.

And then, of course, there are his tools: the endless array of wrenches and screwdrivers in every conceivable size, the boxes of thousands upon thousands of bolts, nails and screws that he has lovingly collected over many years. It doesn't matter that he has never used any of this vital equipment. It is enough for him to spend hours arranging them in alphabetical order or drawing outlines around them where they hang on the wall. (Why do they do this? It seems to be the sort of pointless task given to patients in mental institutions to keep them quietly busy and out of trouble.)

Or perhaps your outwardly ramshackle old shed is hiding a bit of a secret. When was the last time you went in there? It is just possible that behind the splintering

wood, the peeling paint, the cracked and grimy windows – all of which scream, 'Women! Keep Away!' – lies a Neverland for grown-up Peter Pans, complete with plasma screen TVs and minibars. In which case, perhaps it's time we reclaimed these outhouses for ourselves, with the help of a lick of paint and a few cushions here and there and an upgrade from 'shed' to 'summerhouse', a surefire way to enrage the sheddist in your life and ensure that you too can escape from the stresses and strains of daily life.

Shopping

For many of us women, shopping is a recreational activity, best done alone or in the company of other women, who understand that trying on twenty pairs of shoes in five different shops and then buying the first pair we saw is a practical way of ensuring maximum satisfaction with our purchase and not a heinous crime worthy of many hours of whingeing and moaning. Unfortunately, we must occasionally take our menfolk along with us on our retail-therapy jaunts, an experience which, more often that not, is painful and acrimonious.

It starts off OK. You take him first to buy something he claims he desperately needs –a spectacle holder for the car, a plasma TV for his shed – hoping to coax him into a good mood that will last for the duration of your shopping trip. He bounds enthusiastically into the store, bright-eyed and alert, taking his time comparing prices and talking to the sales staff. You are pleased and proud of his negotiating skills. 'Hmm,' you think to yourself. 'Perhaps it won't be so bad this time.' You are mistaken.

Once he has bought his coveted item, it all starts to go downhill. You need to buy some items of clothing, so off you head to the nearest fashion emporium. As you approach the store, you notice that his demeanour is changing. Before he was striding down the street, a happy smile on his face. Now the smile has been replaced by a sulky look and his pace is slowing. Slower and slower he goes, until he is shuffling at snail's pace down the road, the picture of dejected schoolboy misery. 'Come on, get a move on!' you snap. 'We'll be here all day at this rate.' At this he looks alarmed and his pace picks up a bit, but only a bit.

You eventually make it through the doors and head for the sales racks. After a few minutes of browsing, you pick out a nice skirt. 'What do you think of this?' you ask. But you are talking to thin air, because he isn't there. Looking around, you spot him still hovering half-in and half-out of the door, looking out of place and being eyed suspiciously by a burly security guard. You beckon him over and he reluctantly shuffles towards you.

'What are you doing? You're supposed to be helping me. What do you think of this skirt?'

'Lovely. Very nice. Just get that and let's go.'

'But I need to try it on first, and we need to get other stuff too!'

At this he gives a tragic sigh, as if someone's just told him that he has six months to live.

You move about the shop for a while, looking through the various racks, and all the time he follows you around, never venturing more than a foot or two from your side, clearly afraid of getting lost in the terrible and bewildering world of Women's Casual Wear. The frequency and volume of his sighs are increasing and, though you are trying your best to ignore him, out of the corner of your eye you can see him glancing at his watch every few seconds. You are quickly becoming irritated.

'You need some new socks. Why don't you go to the men's department and pick some out?'

He looks frightened. 'Can't you come with me?'

'It'll be quicker if you go by yourself while I finish up here.'

Off he shuffles, eyes cast down to the ground lest he catch the eye of a female shopper while looking at lingerie and be branded a pervert. Thirty seconds later you nearly jump out of your skin when you turn around and find him standing there again, inches away from your face.

'That was quick! Did you get the socks?'

'I couldn't find any. They don't have any.'

'Don't be stupid! Of course they have socks. You just didn't look properly.'

He's got that stubborn look you hate on his face. 'Did look. Couldn't find.' His speech is deteriorating. A bad sign.

You take a deep breath and, struggling to control your temper, lead him off to find his socks. Job done, you head off to the changing rooms, where he joins the ranks of equally pathetic-looking men sitting awkwardly on the row of chairs placed outside. They are not speaking to each other or making eye contact, but you can sense the unspoken bond that exists between them. They are united in their misery.

You join the queue to pay for your purchases and he tugs at your sleeve, like a small child. 'I'm hungry,' he whines. Of course he is. When out shopping, men need to be fed every two hours, like Tamagotchis.

'But we're not finished yet. I've just got to buy a new pair of work shoes and then we'll get something to eat.'

'But I'm starving!' he insists. He looks as if he's about to cry.

You've had enough. 'OK, then. Why don't you go to McDonald's while I buy the shoes and I'll meet you there.'

You watch him head off down the street and the change in him is palpable. His back straightens, his head is held high and the slow, shuffling pace picks up until he is once more striding happily down the street. It's like watching Kevin Spacey's transformation at the end of *The Usual Suspects*.

When it comes to shopping for food, men are more enthusiastic, but they are still more of a hindrance than a help. A fascinating experiment carried out by a boffin at Yale University has proven what we have always known to be true: women are better at shopping than men, particularly when it comes to food. Groups of men and women were taken around a large farmers' market, going from stall to stall, tasting various different foods. They were then taken to the middle of the market and asked to point in the direction of individual stalls. The women were significantly better at this task than the men, although it is generally agreed that men have a better sense of direction. Not only this, but the higher the nutritional value of the food sold by a stall, the more accurately were they able to point it out. This is thought to be a throwback to the hunter/gatherer division between the sexes. Men are better at killing things (orcs, on the PlayStation); women are better at gathering other resources (a sensible weekly shop at Sainsbury's).

It is bad enough when they accompany you to the supermarket. You march efficiently up and down the aisles, planning the week's menus in your head, checking labels for nutritional content and organic guarantees, virtuously whizzing past the crisps and sweets aisles at top speed in order to avoid temptation. Then you reach the checkout and begin to unload the food and…Oh! Wait! You must have mistakenly swapped trolleys with someone else, because this is not what you have carefully selected. But look again more closely, and take a look at your man, who is looking decidedly shifty and is not quite able to meet your eye. You'll find that this is indeed your trolley. It's just that, unbeknown to you, your man has been surreptitiously crossing off items from his own fantasy shopping wish list, one that consists entirely of E-numbers, colossal amounts of saturated fat and sugar, and beer.

Asking a man to do some food shopping on his own, completely unsupervised, is a recipe for disaster. Men are unable to correctly decipher a shopping list, no matter how explicitly written it is. Nor are they able to satisfactorily replace one product with another similar one should they not find exactly what you have requested.

Say, for example, you are planning to cook a paella and send your man off to purchase a few missing ingredients at the last minute. (A dire mistake, one that you will bitterly regret. When will you ever learn?)

You need	*He will buy*
Whole baby squid	Crab sticks
Fresh haddock	A tin of pilchards in tomato sauce
Chorizo	A pack of frozen economy sausages
Short-grain Spanish rice	Boil-in-the-bag Basmati
Saffron	Beer (he panicked)

Family Man

DIY

'A happy man is a man with a Black & Decker power drill,' Confucius once said. Well, OK, he didn't. But he would have done if ancient China had been blessed with a B&Q or Homebase on every street corner.

With television schedules crammed with nearly as many programmes about home improvement as about cars (see Cars), our national obsession with DIY has reached new, feverish heights. Incredibly, a recent survey carried out by the Federation of Master Builders claims that 40 per cent of Brits attempt to carry out all their building and home improvement work themselves, as a result of which we spend around £850m a year on paying professionals to sort out our DIY disasters. It seems that watching half an hour of Nick Knowles fannying about with pieces of MDF makes men think that they are fully able to rewire a house in one afternoon or fit a new kitchen during half-time. In fact, according to the same survey, one in five men claimed they could do a better job than the professionals. One in five!

A little knowledge is a dangerous thing. Take, for example, the case of the Leicester man who shot himself in the heart with a nail gun while attempting to lay some floorboards. The nail actually penetrated his heart, but he wasn't unduly worried until he tried to take off his jumper and realised that it was nailed to his body. He eventually called the emergency services, but not before considering removing the nail himself with a pair of pliers. Or how about the man who set fire to himself after having the inspired idea of removing bathroom tiles with the aid of some paraffin and a blowtorch?

Quite apart from the risk to life and limb, attempting complex DIY jobs is a surefire way to cause untold damage to your home. According to the Woolwich, one in six insurance claims is the result of a botched job, generally resulting in damage to property caused by dropped tools, water damage caused by nails hammered into pipes, feet going through the floor of the loft and fire damage caused by over-enthusiastic amateur welders.

But unfortunately these cautionary tales do little to steer men away from the wonders and temptations of the local branch of Homebase. If you haven't spent at least two Saturday mornings in the past month wandering up and down the aisles, eyes on stalks and heart in mouth as tool after unidentifiable tool finds its way into the shopping trolley, you are a very lucky woman. And as for Ikea – don't even get me started on that.

Actually, yes, do. It's my personal belief that Ikea was invented by the devil himself, in order to cram as much chaos and misery as possible into a Sunday afternoon. If you manage to get through a visit to Ikea without resorting to tears, tantrums and mentions of divorce courts, then well done you. Congratulations.

Negotiating the maze that is the display area is bad enough, what with the out-of-control children bouncing off the walls, the bickering couples and the large family groups with no sense of direction or personal space. Then you have to wander up and down hundreds of badly laid out, dimly lit aisles trying to find the items you want to take to the checkout, where you stand in line for half an hour before realising that the bag of 4,000 screws you need to construct your shelves are sold separately and you have to return to the aisles and start again.

But it is when you return home, tearful and exhausted, that the real fun and games begin. The whole point of flat-pack furniture is that it should be simple to put together, is it not? You should be able to quickly and efficiently screw together a few bits of wood to form a basic bookshelf in one afternoon with the minimum of fuss, even if you don't have a degree in engineering, should you not? Not according to Ikea, you shouldn't. Even the most experienced of DIY-ers will have great difficulty making head or tail of the poorly written instructions with their baffling drawings of parts that look nothing like the parts you have spread out in front of you. And if said DIY-er is a man, with his own unique vision of how to put furniture together, things are bound to go to hell in a handbasket.

Men don't like following instructions. Women will look at an instruction manual and think: 'Hmm, this manual is not very clear. What language is it in and what on earth is that squiggly drawing supposed to be? Is it an earthworm? I knew we should have picked up that bag of earthworms from Aisle 4867776B! Am I even holding this thing the right way up? Oh well, I'd better study it for a while and do my best to follow the directions, or we'll never get these shelves up.'

Men, on the other hand, will look at an instruction manual and think: 'This was written by another man. A man who is trying to TELL ME WHAT TO DO! I won't have my manhood questioned in such a manner. I won't have it, do you hear me, instruction manual? I will put up this bookshelf in my own way, or die trying.'

The solution to all this DIY madness is quite simple: let them get on with it and when they have made enough of a mess of it and have gone off to their sheds to sulk, reach for the Yellow Pages and call in the professionals.

⊙⊙⊙⊙⊙⊙⊙⊙⊙⊙⊙⊙⊙⊙⊙⊙⊙⊙⊙

Common DIY problems and their solutions

Question: I want to add a second sink to the bathroom. How do I extend the existing pipes?
Answer: Call a plumber.

Question: I want to install an electrical outlet in the garage. What is the best way to go about it?
Answer: Call an electrician.

Question: I need to rewire/replumb the entire

house. Should I attempt this myself?

Answer: No! For the love of God, no!

⊙⌒⊙⌒⊙⌒⊙⌒⊙⌒⊙⌒⊙⌒⊙⌒⊙⌒⊙⌒⊙⌒⊙⌒⊙⌒⊙

Teenagers

The teenage boy is a unique creature, an exotic, elusive and sometimes dangerous animal. There is still much for scientists and casual observers to discover about the characteristics and habits of the teenage boy, but certain universal traits have been studied and recorded as follows.

Physical characteristics

Despite having evolved the ability to walk on two legs along with the rest of the human species, it is clear that the teenage boy is more closely related to our ape ancestors than the rest of us. Observe the way he moves about. See how long his arms are, not quite in proportion to the rest of his body. His knuckles are considerably closer to the ground than ours. His gait is highly unique and instantly recognisable – the painfully slow shuffle, the stooped shoulders, the downcast eyes – and it becomes increasingly pronounced the more upset and threatened he feels, an almost permanent condition in fact, because the teenage boy is the most highly sensitive and easily disturbed member of the animal kingdom.

The teenage boy is given to periodic outbursts of virulent oozing pustules, which can appear all over the body, but are particularly to be found on the face, exacerbated by the greasy hair that usually hangs in limp fronds over the forehead and eyes, thus shielding this shy creature from the gaze of curious passers-by. The pustules may look alarming, even a little disgusting, but they are in fact a blessing from Mother Nature, as they put paid to any possible interest from the opposite sex until he has gained a few qualifications, thus protecting him from early fatherhood and a lifetime of minimum-wage jobs at McDonald's.

Contrary to popular belief, the teenage boy does have opposable thumbs, but at this stage in his life they are weak and not properly functioning, thus explaining his inability to hold on to any object for more than a few seconds without sending it crashing to the ground. This clumsiness can be seen in many of his actions, particularly when he walks, as he trips every few paces. This is in part due to the teenage boy's preference for ill-fitting trousers which come down right over his feet, so that they trail along the ground impeding his movements, and fail to adequately cover his backside. It is pitiful to see this poor creature stumbling shambolically along, and you may be tempted to help it out by tugging the trousers up to their correct position. Please do not do this. These volatile creatures should be studied but not approached directly unless you are a trained professional.

Habitat

The teenage boy is not quite a nocturnal creature, but he is rarely to be seen before midday, preferring to spend the early hours buried under mounds of grubby duvets deep within his lair. Indeed, he seldom emerges from his natural habitat, making the occasional foray into the outside world only to feed or socialise with his peers. Not many people have the stomach to enter the teenage boy's private domain, but those intrepid explorers who have taken their lives into their own hands and ventured within can attest to the fact that it is not a pleasant place to be.

Fresh air is fatal to the teenage boy, thus the windows are usually tightly closed and a distinctive and overwhelming stench prevails. Smell is the main defence mechanism of the teenage boy. He gives off a powerful odour, ensuring that his enemies are kept at bay and the privacy of his lair remains intact. Much like fresh air, water and soap are therefore assiduously avoided, and on the rare occasions that the teenage boy is forced to wash himself, he will try to recreate his defensive aura of noxious smells by liberally dousing himself with nasty cheap body sprays and aftershaves.

The lair itself is usually pitch-black, an aversion to sunlight being another trait of the teenage boy. If you dare to peer into the gloom, though, you may spot some alarming items. That crumpled heap in the corner is where the teenage boy sheds his clothes before retiring for the night; when he awakes he will just reach into the pile and pull out random garments, which he will sniff to check that the odour is sufficiently strong to afford him protection throughout the day. Underneath the bed, you will find heaps upon heaps of mugs, plates and cutlery, all sporting green mould in various stages of growth. You may also find piles of magazines, but it is best not to look too closely at these. There will also generally be many items of expensive electrical equipment in the lair, all of which are necessary to and fiercely guarded by the teenage boy. The most precious of these items is his games console, which is vital to him as it allows him to spend hours building up the muscles in his opposable thumbs so that eventually he can stop breaking things.

Communication

Although the snarls, grunts and growls emitted by teenage boys may initially sound like gibberish, it is possible to decipher them and thus you can communicate with these creatures on a basic, primitive level, should you wish to do so. If in doubt, refer to this list of commonly used sounds and their definitions.

ᕬᕬᕬᕬᕬᕬᕬᕬᕬᕬᕬᕬᕬᕬᕬᕬᕬᕬᕬᕬᕬ

'Unhhh?' – An exclamation of surprise. Often heard when a teenage boy is roused from his slumber at an inappropriate hour. This grunting noise will soon be followed by similar but louder and angrier grunts if he is not left alone. This is a bad sign. The best thing to do is just back slowly out of the door and retreat to a safe distance.

'Duh!' – This is an expression of scorn and is often accompanied by plenty of eye-rolling. You have done or said something displeasing to him and he is saying, 'You are unbelievably, criminally stupid. I want nothing to do with you.'

'Dunno!' – This exclamation will be accompanied

by frantic shoulder-shrugging and a few huffs and puffs. It is most likely to be heard when you have asked him a perfectly reasonable question – like 'Why were you home two hours past your curfew last night?' – which he does not want to answer.

Cooking

Gordon Ramsay is quite possibly the most macho man on the planet. He used to be a professional footballer; he has a face that looks like it was carved out of solid granite, yet still manages to be ruggedly attractive; he swears a lot; he has about four million children; he is a hugely successful businessman; his feet are so enormous, he has to have his shoes custom-made; and…he cooks! Gordon and fellow celebrity chefs such as Rick Stein, Jean-Christophe Novelli and Nigel Slater have done much in recent years to encourage the average man into the kitchen. (Note the deliberate exclusion of Jamie Oliver from this list. He almost got a mention, but a quick survey of a few male friends revealed that rather than inspiring them to whip up a romantic meal for two, he just makes them want to smash his face in.)

Is this a good thing? It's not clear. On the one hand,

anything that encourages men to take on more responsibility for some of the day-to-day drudgery that has traditionally fallen to the lot of women has to be a good thing. On the other hand…well, they are men, so things don't always go as smoothly as they should.

There are two types of men when it comes to the culinary arts: a) those to whom cooking is one of the world's greatest mysteries, and b) those who approach the preparation of a meal as if they were about to paint the ceiling of the Sistine Chapel.

In the first category are those men who never managed to progress from their student days, when a typical meal consisted of a Pot Noodle and a few pieces of burnt toast. Take a look in any male student's fridge (having donned a full hazmat suit first, of course) and you'll see what I mean. You are unlikely to find anything even vaguely nutritional in there, and certainly nothing that needs more preparation than a quick blast in the microwave. As for fruit and vegetables: not a chance. The only green things to pass their lips are the odd nasty crisp and past-its-sell-by-date pork pie. It's a miracle so many men manage to graduate from university without contracting scurvy or rickets.

In later years, many of these student throwbacks are concerned enough about their rapidly hardening arteries to improve their diet somewhat, but not by much. They may consent to a bit of lettuce in their kebabs or some mushy peas with their fish and chips. Some may widen their culinary repertoires by finally figuring out how to heat up a tin of baked beans or fry a couple of sausages, but on the whole they tend to stay as far away from the kitchen as possible, as if it were some frightening and sinister parallel universe, populated by fierce dragons who might at any moment emerge from the oven and evil trolls who live in the dishwasher. While it is depressing to cook day after day for a man who you know full well would much rather be chowing down on a chicken tikka Masala from the local takeaway, it is preferable to being lumbered with the second type of man: he who sees cooking as an Art Form.

The problem with men who like to cook is that they do not see cooking as a necessary chore. They do not feel it is their job to produce a nutritionally balanced, tasty, economical meal for the entire family every night of the week. That is still women's work. For them, cooking is a hobby, one indulged in only when they can be sure there will be an appreciative audience. It is a massive production, an all-singing, all-dancing, multi-million-pound West End show, starring one of the Osmonds.

This type of man will only cook for dinner parties.

Starter

Cappuccino of Morels with a Drizzle of Mint Jus

Main Course

Miso-crusted Veal with a Truffle Oil Sorbet,
served with a Pomme-de-Terre Fondant
and Seaweed

Dessert

Crème Glacée à la Fraise with
Lemongrass-and-Grapefruit-Infused Shortbread

He will dream up a menu so elaborate and pretentious that is virtually impossible to figure out exactly what you will be eating.

Preparations usually commence many, many hours before the guests arrive, usually early in the morning, thus precluding anyone else from preparing any other food in the kitchen that day. First comes the gathering together of vital kitchen equipment, which basically means every single pot, pan, knife, chopping board, mixing bowl and wooden spoon. Every useless kitchen gadget you have ever misguidedly bought will be brought out of the Kitchen Gadget Graveyard, dusted off and laid out for use. For, make no mistake about it, he will use every single item you possess. At the end of the evening, you would be forgiven for thinking that the SAS had just conducted a search-and-destroy mission in your previously spotlessly clean, beautifully uncluttered kitchen. As you wearily begin to clean up after him, you will wonder what on earth he could have used the pasta machine for when there was no pasta on the menu (to your knowledge; to be fair, it was hard to tell). And why are there bits of meat in the juicer? Surely he couldn't have used it to make the gravy (but he probably did).

After fifteen solid hours of intense culinary activity, during which you will no doubt be hovering anxiously outside the closed kitchen door, fruitlessly pleading for

him to allow you entrance so that you can practise a bit of damage limitation, the guests will arrive. You will take coats, pour drinks and then spend the next few hours awkwardly trying to talk over the clattering, banging and roars of rage and frustration coming from the kitchen.

By the time the meal is served, just before midnight, your guests will be so drunk and famished that they will happily wolf down whatever is on offer, thus giving your man the false confidence to plan yet another dinner party for next week. Oh joy.

Housework

Once upon a time, in a land far, far away, there existed a kingdom of blissful tranquillity. The inhabitants of this magical place spent their days in pursuit of pleasure, doing whatever their hearts desired. They would wake up early in the morning and cook themselves a huge breakfast, leaving the greasy pots and pans on the hob and blobs of ketchup all over the counter. Then they would go for a leisurely walk around their green and pleasant fiefdom, perhaps stopping for a picnic lunch and a frolic in the fields. They would return home, tired and happy, and traipse muddy footprints all over the house. After a couple of hours of playing with their adorable children, they would slope off to bed, leaving toys all over the living-room floor and a trail of discarded clothes on the stairs. No thought of tidying up after themselves crossed their minds, but no matter! For late at night, when the household was sound asleep, the washing-up fairy, vacuum-cleaning elf and polishing pixie would spring into action and the next morning they would awake to find everything sparkling and fresh once more.

But things soon took a turn for the worse. The washing-up fairy hung up her tiny, fairy-sized Marigolds in disgust when she eventually realised what a selfish, thoughtless lot the inhabitants of this kingdom were. The vacuum-cleaning elf demanded to be paid for his hard labour and when nothing was forthcoming he persuaded the polishing pixie to run away with him in a quest to find a home where they would be appreciated and

rewarded. And so this once-peaceful, sunny kingdom became a dark place of misery, drudgery and terrible rows about whose turn it was to take the bin out.

Unfortunately for us women, many men have enormous difficulty in separating the fairy tale from reality. In their minds, the washing-up fairy, vacuum-cleaning elf and polishing pixie are still feverishly working away behind the scenes, ensuring that their homes are pristine at all times and their clothes are washed, ironed and put neatly away.

We are in a catch-22 situation. On the one hand, we rightly feel it is absurdly unfair that the brunt of the household chores should fall to us; on the other hand, if we know that the chores we delegate to our other halves will be done sloppily, accompanied by much whingeing and moaning and stomping of feet, or not at all, and we don't want to live in a filthy hovel, then we have no choice but to roll up our sleeves and get on with it ourselves.

So what is exactly is their problem when it comes to domestic chores? Here are several theories.

The Oedipus complex

Some men just want to be shacked up with women who are like their mothers. Not in a pervy, go-directly-to-jail way, but men of a certain age were brought up in households where their mothers slaved away all day, cooking, cleaning, washing, ironing, folding, tidying and scrubbing, while their fathers waltzed merrily off to work, where they sat around faffing about with bits of paper and ogling secretaries before heading off to the pub. On arriving home, they were greeted by a smiling wife in a pretty frock and a three-course gourmet meal. It must have been a bit of a shock to the system when these men grew up and realised that times had changed, women had fled from their kitchens straight to the boardrooms and they were now expected to do their fair share of the household chores. They cannot accept the new status quo, and so they stubbornly bury their heads in the sand, refusing to believe that the 1950s male utopia, when an iron was simply a stick with which to hit balls into small holes and a clothes horse was a well-dressed blonde with big boobs, is dead and buried.

Preposition confusion

Scientists have recently discovered that the male brain is unable to correctly translate words such as 'on' and 'in'. Well, OK, I made that up. But should a boffin ever have the foresight to conduct such a research project he – or, more likely, she – will discover that this phenomenon is indeed a reality. You see, women know that dirty dishes go *in* the dishwasher. This is pure, simple logic and common sense. Men, however, cannot grasp this fact. They know it deep down, but when it comes to actually performing the deed, their poorly wired brains insist that the plates should actually be left *on* the dishwasher. The same is true when it comes to the laundry, only things become slightly more complicated in this case because words such as 'around' and 'nearby' come into play. The dirty washing should go *in* the laundry basket, not *on* it, scattered *around* it or *nearby*. They can't help it, though. They just don't have the necessary brainpower, the poor things.

Dirt-blindness

Again, this is a phenomenon that is down to bad genetics or a brain deficiency or something, so we cannot blame them for this. We can only pity them. When a woman looks at, say, a kitchen floor, she will see a stomach-churningly revolting mass of muddy footprints, crumbs and unidentifiable, sinister-looking stains, teeming with deadly bacteria that must be dealt with immediately. A man will look at the same floor and see a gleaming, sparkling surface so sanitary that you could, should the need arise, perform emergency open-heart surgery on it.

The Inability to Digest Instructions or Operate Technology

A bit of a mouthful this one, isn't it? Let's just call it the IDIOT syndrome. It doesn't matter if your other half is a rocket scientist working for NASA who spends his spare time constructing banana-skin-fuelled cars out of matchsticks and bits of tinfoil, when faced with a dial and a row of five buttons on the washing machine he will stand there staring at it, seemingly mesmerised by the sheer complexity of it all. No matter how many times you've explained the process to him, he will ask you the same questions – 'Which button do I press?', 'What does this thingamigig here do?', 'Where do I put the washing powder?' – until you scream with rage and frustration, grab the load of laundry and do it yourself. Which is, of course, exactly what he wants.

So there you have it; those are the theories. But what can be done about this male versus female stand-off? It seems that there is no easy solution, but we could perhaps look to Spain for some inspiration. Men in Spain are traditionally so macho that asking them to do a spot of ironing is akin to suggesting they cut off their testicles, so MPs have drawn up a voluntary marriage contract which legally obliges men to take on their fair share of the housework and childcare.

Furthermore, a Spanish inventor has come up with a couple of ingenious gadgets in an attempt to persuade or coerce Spanish men to help out around the house: a washing machine which uses fingerprint technology to ensure that the same person cannot use it twice in a row and an iron which contains heavy weights, so that you can build up a bit of muscle every time you iron your shirts. *Viva España*!

Toilet habits

The Great Toilet Seat War

The year is 1775. Intrepid English watchmaker and inventor of the world's first flushing toilet Alexander Cummings is extolling the wonders of this m o d e r n device to a female customer.

'And so you see, madam, this is truly a revolutionary invention. No longer will you have to pee into dainty but inadequate little pots in the middle of the night! No longer will you have to deal with malodorous wet trails all along the hallway as your clumsy servants slosh their way downstairs to empty them! No, for all your business will be automatically flushed down into the street where it belongs, with no inconvenience to anyone.'

'Except for the poor people who live on the streets.'

'Yes, except for them. But we don't care about the poor people.'

'Hmm. Very clever. What else does this thing do?'

'Well, madam, this device has been designed to provide maximum convenience to both the male and female members of the household. Behold this handy seat. When it is up, in its correct position, the toilet is ready to be used by gentlemen. When a lady needs to answer the call of nature, she simply lowers the seat and positions herself upon it in the greatest of comfort. As long as she then remembers to put the seat up again.'

'Hang on a minute. Surely the correct position for this seat thingy is down? Is it not beholden on the gentleman to lower it after he has finished his business? You cannot expect a lady such as myself to have to lay her delicate hands on any part of this contraption after her husband has had a go on it. His aim has not been improved by a lifetime of peeing into the little pots, you know.'

'Madam, surely you jest! The seat must remain by default in the upright position! It takes far more effort to lift the seat up than it does to put it down. It's the only way that makes sense.'

'But it doesn't make sense at all! I'm not the one who is going to be weeing erratically all over the place, leaving nasty wet droplets everywhere. Why should I be the one to have to touch the horrid thing? And, anyway, shouldn't both the seat and the lid be down before flushing commences? Otherwise there is danger of splashback and thus germs being sprayed all over the place.'

'You weren't worried about the germs when you were peeing in the little pots and storing them under your bed, were you? I fail to see the logic in your argument, madam.'

And thus began the Great Toilet Seat War, a vicious war that has been waged between men and women the world over ever since, one which shows no sign of abating. It is not a war that can be easily settled, after all. There is not much room for compromise – the seat cannot be half up and half down; it must be one or the other – and so there is no starting point upon which a lengthy period of peace talks can be based.

Interestingly, extensive research into this particular aspect of the battle of the sexes has shown that men are much more troubled by the 'up or down' debate than women. Yes, we whinge and moan with our female friends, sharing horror stories of the time we nearly fell into the lavatory bowl in the middle of the night and flushed ourselves into the sewers. We nag our men about the issue on a fairly regular basis, throwing around a few threats and accusations for good measure, although much good it does us.

But it's men who really take the issue to heart. They write articles and pleading letters to etiquette advice columns about it. They post long, impassioned rants about it on message boards. It seems that we women are committing an unspeakable, unforgivable sin by asking them to please, out of courtesy and thoughtfulness, put the loo seat down when they are finished in there. Yes, indeed, we are evil, selfish creatures to demand such a terrible thing from our menfolk. How dare we!

Take a look on the Internet and you will find several studies on the topic, all written by men. These are actual scientific studies written by actual scientists with lots of letters after their names, complete with pages and pages of mind-numbingly complicated equations to do with inconvenience caused and effort exerted. They even have footnotes and bibliographies. It may surprise you that these scientists have chosen to work in the loo-seat field of research when there is cancer to cure and world hunger to end, but it will surely not come as a surprise to learn that every single one of these studies concludes that the toilet seat should be left up. 'This is our conclusion and we have proved it without doubt by bamboozling you with maths. There can be no further argument.'

But, yes, there can. Let's attempt to settle this matter once and for all, using good old-fashioned common sense. Although it is undoubtedly an improvement on the little pots, the toilet is not an object of great cleanliness, no matter how diligently you scrub and disinfect it. Nasty things go into it and therefore it stands to reason that nasty things come out of it. When you flush and then stand at the sink next to the loo, brushing your teeth or putting on some make-up, you are actually being liberally sprayed with microscopic droplets of water, germs and other unmentionable things. And so, as Alexander Cummings's argumentative female customer so wisely pointed out, the lid of the loo should really be down whenever it is not in use, for reasons of hygiene, aesthetics and to stop the dog from drinking out of it. If the lid is down, then the seat is also down.

There you go. Conflict resolved and Nobel Peace Prize due any day now.

∽∾∽∾∽∾∽∾∽∾∽∾∽∾∽∾∽∾∽∾∽∾

Toilet etiquette 101 – a basic course for the lavatorially challenged gentleman

Lesson one

'A German man and an Englishman are standing at the urinals. The Englishman finishes up and heads straight for the bathroom door, whereupon the German says, "In Germany they teach us to wash our hands." The Englishman replies, "In England they teach us not to pee on them."'

Are you one of those men who chirp up with one of the many variations of this old joke when confronted by someone who has cottoned on to the fact that you have waltzed straight out of the loo, hands dry as a bone and no damp towel or paper napkin in sight? If so, please just think for a moment about what you are saying. Are you really suggesting that there is no need to spend five seconds of your valuable time washing your hands because you have not actually, deliberately *peed on them*? Are you out of your mind, sir?

See this square bar of sweet-smelling stuff here by the sink? This is called soap. See this wet, transparent matter that miraculously appears out of the metal thing when you turn this knob? This is called water. Water and soap are your friends; please use them.

Lesson two

'Water, water everywhere, nor any drop to drink.' Samuel Taylor Coleridge may have been talking about mariners adrift in the middle of the ocean when he penned these words, but he could just as easily have been thinking about the state some of you men leave the bathroom in.

Any rogue drops of water in the bathroom should come from the various taps, not from your good selves. Why must you sprinkle when you tinkle? You have been dealing with the complexities of your male equipment since the day you were born, so why is it that you are still unable to aim properly? It's ironic, really, because in the winter months, when you are three sheets to the wind,

you have no difficulty in writing your name in
the snow with amazing clarity and even a few
calligraphic swirls and flourishes.

If things do not improve in this area drastic
measures will have to be taken. Think of the poor
men of Germany who are being forced to wee
sitting down by an ingenious little gadget which
sits under the seat. An alarm is triggered whenever
the seat is lifted and a disembodied voice with a
creepy fake American accent intones: 'Don't you
go wetting this floor, cowboy, you never know
who's behind you. So sit down and get your water
pistol in the bowl where it belongs. Ha, ha, ha.'
That happens *every single time* you lift the seat.
Think about that. Lesson learned? Good.

Lesson three
This is a simple lesson: the bathroom bin won't
empty itself. No, really, it won't, no matter how
expensive and shiny it is. We all long for the day
when our household appliances are so high-tech
that they have minds of their own and will clean
and polish and empty themselves without any
input from us (although it would be quite
disconcerting to bump into the vacuum cleaner

wheeling itself down the hallway to meet up with
the food processor for some sort of secret tryst).
Unfortunately, that day is still far in the future.
For now, it would be nice if you could stop trying
to create your very own miniature version of
the Leaning Tower of Pisa in the bathroom.
We understand that there is a certain kind of
fascination in spending a good chunk of the
already considerable time you spend in the toilet
trying to balance just one more empty shampoo
bottle or loo roll on top of the precarious pile of
assorted bathroom debris. Hobbies are good –
we encourage you to have as many as possible,
to keep you busy and out of mischief – but please
try to find something more constructive to do with
your spare time.

∞∞∞∞∞∞∞∞∞∞∞∞∞∞∞∞∞∞∞∞∞∞

Playground of the Gods

The average British male spends up to three years of his
life in the loo; women manage to conduct their bathroom
business in the more reasonable period of just one year.
Like the humble but much revered shed, the smallest
room in the house is something of a refuge for men. It is

a place of calm and contemplation, much like a Japanese Zen garden. There they can sit on the loo for many happy hours, thumbing through their old copies of *Playboy* (bought 'for the articles', of course), safe in the knowledge that most females would rather run naked down the high street on a busy Saturday afternoon than venture within when the male of the house is ensconced upon the porcelain throne. In this matter they are rather like those animals, such as skunks, that emit vile and deadly odours and gases when under duress, to keep their enemies at bay. Mother Nature is indeed a wondrous thing.

If you want to take a quick, incredulous look at some of the devices designed for men to ensure that a couple of hours of bathroom time is more fun than a night out with the lads, see the section on gadgets, but there are some that take their toilet fixations even further.

Take Sim Jae-duck, for example, the Korean man who built an incredibly detailed toilet-shaped mansion which he named 'Haewoojae', which translates as 'a place of sanctuary where one can solve one's worries'. As he holds a lofty position in that great and most useful of organisations, the World Toilet Association, it is perhaps unsurprising that he should have gone with this particular design, but one does wonder about his state of mind.

Then there is the enormously popular chain of toilet-themed restaurants in Taiwan, where customers sit on bogs to eat food (mostly of the brown variety – curries and chocolate ice-cream and the like) out of specially made toilet bowls, which come in two sizes: small (Number One) and large (Number Two). They wipe their hands on loo rolls suspended above the tables, they stare in awe at the lamps made out of urinals – the loo-related fun never ends.

A little closer to home, John Clarke hit the headlines when he turned his bathroom into a male haven. Having promised his fiancée he would spend less time in the pub, he promptly set about recreating the atmosphere of his beloved local in his own loo, equipping it with a wide-screen TV, PlayStation, dartboard, bar snacks and a drinks optic suspended above the bath. Soon his male friends were dropping in to spend time with John in the lav on a regular basis, despite the obvious safety and hygiene issues involved in cramming expensive electronic equipment into a space that is regularly awash with water and eating crisps from a bowl which is in close proximity to a toilet. Shockingly, John's fiancée was not entirely happy with this situation – 'I knew she was annoyed when she had to bring the takeaways in'– and after a few months she left him. 'There's no pleasing some women,' said John.

Parenting

What kind of father is your fella? Does he throw himself wholeheartedly into the role, changing nappies with the kind of dexterity and skill usually only seen in top-notch surgeons in posh private hospitals, and raising his kids with a firm but kind hand? Or does he express shock and dismay when asked to look after his offspring for half an hour and slope out of the house muttering something about 'an important prior arrangement', probably down the pub or at the bookie's? Take this quiz to find out.

1. What was his reaction when you told him you were pregnant? Did he:

a) Burst into tears of joy and spend the next few months regaling friends and family/neighbours/ the postman/strangers on the street with tales of how 'our pregnancy' was progressing in minute and gruesome detail.

b) Turn pale and start to shake like a leaf, spend a few sleepless nights worrying about money and how often he would be able to escape to the pub when the baby was born, but then get used to the idea and feel cautiously pleased about it.

c) Stare at you in horror for a few moments, then

leg it out of the house with the speed and grace of a gazelle to 'buy a pack of cigarettes', never to be seen again.

2. Where was he when you gave birth?

a) Right there with you, holding your hand, telling you to 'breathe through the pain' and insisting to any doctor who tried to get near you that 'we' want a natural birth with minimum intervention, until you were belting him round the head with any hospital equipment you could get your hands on and using the kind of language only heard down the docks or at a Billy Connolly live show.

b) He was there, but spent most of the time cowering pathetically in a corner in the foetal position, rocking backwards and forwards and moaning louder than you were. Then, when he did eventually dare to take a peek at what was going on, he promptly passed out, necessitating the attentions of the entire medical team, thus leaving you to struggle on alone.

c) He was down the pub with his mates, although he did occasionally send a text message exhorting you to 'Push!'

**3. You both manage to fit in a rare night out
and return home to find the house in utter
chaos, the babysitter bound and gagged and
locked in the broom cupboard and the cat
shaved and dyed an alarming shade of purple.
What does he do?**

a) He immediately takes charge of the situation.
   He calms the babysitter down and persuades
   her not to go to the police, then gives the kids
   a stern talking-to and organises them into an
   efficient cleaning-up team.

b) He hovers in the doorway, unsure what to
   do, and watches you deal with the situation,
   occasionally coming up with impractical and
   unhelpful advice, until you tell him to go away,
   whereupon he retreats to the safety of his shed
   with a stiff drink to calm his nerves.

c) He laughs uproariously and congratulates the
   kids on their creative mischief-making skills.

**4. You ask him to look after the kids for the
afternoon while you treat yourself to some
much-needed retail therapy. On your return,
what do you find?**

a) They are all gathered around the kitchen table,

constructing an energy-efficient wind turbine
out of organic yoghurt pots and loo rolls and
snacking on freshly baked sugar-free, fat-free
brownies.

b) All seems to be well – they are sitting innocently
on the sofa, looking like butter wouldn't melt.
But, suspicious of your man's slightly sheepish
look, you do a bit of reconnaissance and soon
discover a hidden cache of crisp and sweet
wrappers and an empty bottle of cola, which
means the kids will be bouncing off the walls
all night long.

c) The kids are plonked down in front of the telly
watching *The Exorcist* on DVD and your man is
at the bottom of the garden, flirting with the
next-door neighbour over the fence.

**5. Your son is playing in his school's under-nines
football team against their deadly rivals, Bash
Street Juniors. To your horror, your son performs
a vicious and uncalled-for tackle on another
boy. Does your man:**

a) Immediately remove the child from the pitch
and bar him from participating in any further
matches for the next month, thus teaching him

that violence of any kind is unacceptable.

b) Smirk and look proud until he catches your eye, whereupon he quickly rearranges his features into a suitably disapproving expression.

c) Do a victory jig on the touchline, hollering, 'Go on, my son! That'll teach 'em! In your face, Bash Street Juniors! IN YOUR FACE!'

6. You call your teenage son down for breakfast and he eventually appears accompanied by an attractive young girl who has obviously spent the night. What does your man do?

a) He says nothing at the time and treats the girl with kindness and courtesy, and later he sits your son down for a man-to-man chat about safe sex and household rules.

b) He goes bright red, buries himself behind his newspaper in order to avoid all eye contact and eventually stammers something about rearranging his toolbox and disappears.

c) He greets your son with a flurry of blatantly obvious winks and nudges and fawns and leers all over the poor girl until she looks as if she is about to burst into tears or die of embarrassment.

7. Which of these famous quotes about fatherhood would your man most relate to:

a) 'It's a wise father that knows his own child.'
   William Shakespeare

b) 'To be a successful father, there's one absolute rule: when you have a kid, don't look at it for the first two years.' *Ernest Hemingway*

c) 'Never raise your hand to your kid. It leaves your groin unprotected.' *Red Buttons*

Mostly As

Your man is Charles Ingalls, the wholesome, decent, God-fearing father in *Little House on the Prairie*. Nothing is too much trouble for this man when it comes to his family. He rules his brood firmly but fairly, educating them in the ways of the world and bringing them up to be hard-working, responsible citizens. And all this after spending his days toiling the land and driving the pony and trap to the local town to pick up some lengths of gingham for you. What a hero! Or is he? Has he got any skeletons in his closet? Are you sure? Not even a stray rib or a teeny metacarpal? Double-check, because quite often when something seems too good to be true, it's because it is.

Mostly Bs

D'oh! You've got yourself a Homer Simpson. His
heart is in the right place, but he doesn't quite cut
the mustard when it comes to fulfilling his share of
the childcare duties. There's no doubt that he loves
his kids, but he's also a little bit afraid of them, and
they know it. Kids can smell fear from a mile away,
the way a starving dog can smell a roasting beef joint,
and they show no mercy when it comes to taking
advantage of it. This fear coupled with a not insignificant dollop of laziness means that you are the one
who deals with the day-to-day fallout, while he retreats
to a quiet space with a beer and his newspaper.

Mostly Cs

Oh dear. You have inadvertently chosen to breed
with Anakin Skywalker, aka Darth Vader, arguably
the worst fictional father of them all. What were
you thinking? It is unlikely that your man spends
his days hunting down and killing Jedi Knights, but
nonetheless he is evil incarnate, not the best role
model for children. Your kids have probably
already accumulated several ASBOs between
them, which are no doubt lovingly framed and
hung on the wall by their proud father.

Boys and Their Toys

Gadgets

We will touch on this theme briefly in the section on cars, but it is worth taking a more in-depth tour through the world of Toys for Boys. So strap yourselves in and hang on to your hats, ladies, it's going to be a bumpy ride.

Working in the marketing department of a firm which produces a gadget aimed at men must be the easiest job in the world, for if men have no need of it and can't afford it, they will want it. Add some chrome and a few neon lights and

Bob's your uncle. You are onto a sure-fire winner. It couldn't be simpler.

We're not talking about the flimsy little gizmos that people get given as stocking fillers at Christmas – the remote-controlled fart machines, creepy robot puppies, and so on – that provide a few hours of drunken entertainment and are then relegated to the loft, never to see the light of day again. No, we're talking about the super high-tech, super-expensive gadgets that have men drooling with desire and reaching for their cobwebby wallets, such as the prohibitively expensive fridge that comes complete with MP3 player, digital photo frame, satellite radio and wi-fi message centre. And there you were naively feeling perfectly content with your bog-standard, bargain-basement model which does nothing but keep your food cold.

These days it seems that you are nobody if you don't have a mobile phone that can tell you what the temperature is in Timbuktu at any given moment, pick up your weekly shopping at Sainsbury's, take the kids to school and turn into a speedboat in under two seconds whenever you need to make a quick getaway. In this matter, as in so many others, men have firmly cast aside those pesky, party-pooping parts of their brains that deal with self-control and common sense in favour of gratifying the schoolboy within. Let's take a look at some of the gadgets available.

Licensed to Kill

You don't have to have links with MI5 to buy spy-level equipment any more. Any Tom, Dick or Harry can log on to the Internet and purchase gadgets that would make Q green with envy (any Tom, Dick or Harry with more money than sense, that is). The fictional world of spying has convinced men that it is all about fast cars, cocktails, casinos, beautiful women with not very many clothes on and pens that turn into helicopters. Of course in reality spies lead miserable, paranoid existences wondering whether someone's sneaked some high-grade polonium in with their bacon and eggs.

Bulletproof backpacks

The manufacturer claims, with a totally straight face, that this item is a necessity for 'students, concerned parents and commuters' and goes on to kindly remind us that 'it's a major survival advantage versus not having any protection at all and being shot at with a couple of 9mm rounds'. It probably is, if the shooter was actually aiming at the middle of your back, rather than your head, legs or any other part of your body not protected by this mighty backpack. If you are being regularly ambushed by snipers on your way to work or school, moving house might be a better option.

Spy-camera sunglasses

These little beauties allow you to take high-definition photographs of people without their knowledge, thanks to a teeny little camera and a remote control. This is beyond creepy. If you get your kicks taking surreptitious photographs of people you should either be in jail or working as a paparazzo. Either way, nothing good can come of it. The best thing about this gizmo is the emphatic, large-print message in the product description which states that 'these are NOT X-ray or see-through specs'. It is hilarious, and at the same time terribly sad, that the manufacturer felt the need to make this clear. It seems that grown men have never fully relinquished their schoolboy fantasies that one day X-ray specs will become a reality and they will be able to stroll down the street ogling naked women to their hearts' content, with nobody any the wiser.

Musical tasers

Tasers – the weapon of choice for delivering maximum pain with the minimum of mess and fuss. But don't you sometimes find the anguished screams of your victims a bit off-putting? No worries, though, because this handy item comes equipped with an MP3 player, so you can plug in the latest Girls Aloud single and zap away in blissful tranquillity.

Net shooters

This Spiderman-inspired gadget is apparently indispensable if you regularly 'capture animals or apprehend suspects' in the course of your day-to-day business. If not, it is just another useless, potentially dangerous piece of junk.

Techno Toilets

Unsurprisingly, given that the gadget industry is targeted primarily at men, there is a plethora of gizmos available to help make a trip to the loo as lengthy and enjoyable an experience as possible.

The LavNav nightlight

This is described as a 'visual targeting system' which you attach to your loo seat. It has motion sensors which turn on a sickly green light when someone stumbles into the loo in the dark, thus hopefully putting a stop to the puddles of pee all over the seat and floor due to misdirection. This is quite handy, you might say, a jolly useful invention. Yes, possibly. But there is a cheaper solution to this problem. It's called 'turning on the light'.

Bathroom entertainment systems

For women, a trip to the bathroom is generally just a quick pit stop in order to answer a call of nature or attend to matters of personal hygiene. Yes, we enjoy the odd lengthy soak in the tub with a good book and maybe a glass of wine, but that's as far as it goes. We don't expect to have a rollicking good time in there. We don't expect to be entertained as we wee. Not so men. They have to while away the many hours they spend in there somehow, and in these high-tech days a newspaper or a good book is just not good enough. Nowadays you can turn bathtime into a mini rave with an underwater light show or be serenaded by the musical gizmo which attaches to your loo seat and can be programmed to play 'soothing jazz, Latin guitar, modern techno or even nature sounds like rain, ocean waves or a mountain stream'. Ah, the wonders of modern science!

Toilet nanny

Saving the best for last in this section is the only gadget you should even consider spending your hard-earned cash on, and it was clearly invented by a woman. God bless her, whoever she is! This marvellous device is attached to the loo seat, which when lifted activates a recorded message which states: 'Excuse me, sir. Please try to urinate in the toilet, not on the floor, and put the seat down when you are finished. Thank you.'

For the geek within

It is an undisputed fact that most gadgets are created by geeks for geeks, but some reach such dizzy heights of nerdiness and uselessness that they deserve a category all of their own.

Binary alarm clock

This clock has six columns of lights, with each column representing a number from 0 to 9. The two columns on the left indicate hours, the middle two are minutes and the right two are seconds. So to tell the time in the middle of the night, you just need to work out the value of each column, depending on which lights are on. Simple no? It should only take you an hour or so to figure it out, by which time you will be wide awake, so there's no need to set the alarm function at all. Ingenious!

Power jacket

This has to be the ultimate gadget for geeks who love gadgets. An Australian research team has spent millions of dollars developing a jacket that produces power and stores it, so that you can power up all the thousands of gizmos you just can't live without, without the need to find a socket. If the thought of walking around crackling with electricity, like a human dynamo, is unnerving to you, comfort yourself with the thought that you will look really cool in this extra bulky, extra geeky anorak.

Beer

This isn't your bog-standard twenty-pints-of-lager-a-quick-punch-up-and-a-kebab-on-the-way-home here. No, we're talking Real Ale, the beverage of choice for Real Men, or so they would have you believe.

Real Ale conjures up images of buxom wenches serving up frothy jugs of ale amidst much raucous laughter in a far-off time when men ruled supreme and women were tethered, barefoot and pregnant, to the kitchen sink. It is not, therefore, surprising that the Campaign for Real Ale is the largest single-issue consumer group in the UK, boasting 85,000 members as of 2007, most of which, one could safely wager, are men. The appeal is obvious.

Let's take the suggestive, macho or just downright stupid names as a starting point. These are clearly aimed at men, and men only: Bishop's Finger (snigger), Lion Slayer (I am man, hear me roar), Moose Drool Brown Ale (moose drool? Seriously?), Smuttynose Wheat Wine (who are they kidding? It's still beer) and Locky's Liquor Locker Liquor (try ordering that when you've already had several pints of Nun's Knickers). No woman in her right mind would be caught dead drinking beverages with such ridiculous names. No, we'll stick to our Screaming Orgasms and Sex-on-the-Beaches, thank you very much.

And why are there so many different varieties – literally thousands? To the uneducated female palate, they all taste of the same thing: beer. In a sad attempt to appeal to the female market, breweries have produced flavoured

ales – strawberry, banana, chocolate and the like –
but we are not to be fooled. They still taste of beer. Soft-
drink manufacturers have tried the same tack with not
much more success. When faced with a bewildering
array of different-flavoured colas, we will stick with the
good, old-fashioned plain variety. Maybe lemon or lime.
Not vanilla, though – that's horrid. Men, it seems, are
more easily tricked.

Real Ale enthusiasts justify the fact that they spend far
more time down the pub than they should by snottily
declaring that Real Ale appreciation is a fine art, a
respectable hobby, one that is practised by toffs and
intellectuals, like Inspector Morse. (Perhaps they should
remember that Morse would have lived considerably
longer had he not spent so many hours smoking and
drinking pints in picturesque country pubs, while poor,
dim-witted Lewis plodded around Oxford doing all the
donkey work.) We women know, of course, that this is
a load of old cobblers. It's just an excuse to get pissed
with their mates, and no amount of posturing will
persuade us otherwise.

Imagine, if you dare, time spent with a bunch of Real
Ale enthusiasts. On a day of sampling, the conversation
would probably go something like this:

Ale no. 1: Hmm, yes, this is delightful. Fruity, yet light on the palate.

Ale no. 2: Not bad. There is a pleasant flowery flavour which complements the slightly bitter aftertaste.

Ale no. 5: Interesting. The hops … Oh, look, they've put the football on.

Ale no. 7: Mmmm, beer. Cor, the barmaid looks a bit like Abi Titmuss.

Ale no. 10: Ish marvelloush, alesh are good. Oi, darlin', ten more pintsh of this one and some pork scratchingsh.

Cars

When it comes to choosing a car, women generally have a short, simple list of requirements: it must be able to get you safely from A to B, it must not cost a small fortune to run, it must have a simple-to-operate radio and CD player, it must have a mirror, preferably with a light. That's about it. Of course, we would all be delighted to own a snazzy little sports car, but, really, we're not that fussed. We do not feel that the car we drive is a measure of who we are. We are quite capable of holding our heads up high in public, even though we drive a Nissan Micra and not a Porsche.

For the average man, however, it is a completely different story. 'My car is bigger, faster, shinier, noisier, newer, more expensive than yours. Nyah, nyah, nyah.' Men see their cars as extensions of themselves, says a recent study, 'The Secret Life of Cars and What They Reveal About Us'. (Do cars have secret lives? Do they silently back themselves out of our driveways at night when we are asleep and gather at some underground cars-only club to cross-dress or indulge in a spot of bare-knuckle boxing? Do they perhaps have second families stashed away in the suburbs somewhere? Who knew?) Of course, this is hardly earth-shattering news. It is something we women have known since the very first motorist drove the very first motor car proudly down the street at four miles per hour, striking terror into the hearts of passers-by. We knew then that our relationships with our menfolk would henceforth take second place to the special bond that exists between Man and Car.

So men's fascination with all things vehicular is nothing new. But at least in days gone by they were not encouraged to take this obsession to such dizzy heights. They would perhaps spend some time faffing about under bonnets, then take themselves off to their gentlemen's clubs and discuss the relative merits of motor versus horse and cart with their peers over a glass or two of port. But then, at the end of the day, they would return home to their long-suffering wives and put all thoughts of motoring out of their minds. Unfortunately, this is no longer the case. Turn on the TV of an evening and it's cars, cars, cars, cars and more cars. There are entire channels devoted to them. There is no escape. Much of the blame for this can be laid squarely at the feet of one man: Jeremy Clarkson, we are looking at you, and we are not liking what we see.

Top Gear was amusing for about five minutes. Now it is just infuriating. The sight of a bunch of middle-aged men behaving like overgrown, overexcited schoolboys is enough to drive any woman to screaming point. 'Let's race these ridiculously overpowered cars across the country, with absolutely no regard for road safety!' 'Let's catapult this caravan into a canyon and watch it smash to smithereens, for no discernible reason!' 'Let's try to manoeuvre the most humungous vehicles we can get our hands on into a city-centre underground car park, causing massive tailbacks of enraged motorists trying to go about their daily business, giggling like imbeciles all the while!' 'Let's blow things up!' Grow up already. The other presenters get a pass (especially Richard Hammond, because he is cute, like a little pixie), but Clarkson has a lot to answer for. He is clearly the ringleader. He is the Peter Pan to their Lost Boys.

And the gadgets, oh dear Lord, the gadgets. Here are just a few of the mostly pointless, sometimes baffling car accessories available for men to spend their hard-earned cash on.

Sat Nav

This is all well and good. A useful instrument on the whole. But only if you are actually going to follow the directions it gives you. If you are going to insist that it is 'wrong' or that you know a 'shortcut', why not save yourselves an awful lot of money and consult a map if you lose your way, or – shock, horror – ask for directions like normal people (i.e. women)?

Interior mood lights

Unless your man is planning a romantic date in the back of the car (and if he is, run for the hills), there can be no possible use for this. The only mood to be in when in the car is one of anticipation: anticipating that you will arrive where you want to be in one piece. If, for whatever reason, you are afraid for your life, no amount of clever lighting is going to change that.

Spectacle holders

If you are short-sighted and are driving a car, your spectacles should be ON YOUR FACE, not in a holder.

Do-it-yourself window-tinting kits

It is unlikely that your man is a gangster or a pop star, likely to be mobbed by hordes of screaming fans or apprehended by the police whenever he sets foot outside the house. In which case, he does not need tinted windows.

Quickshift filters

Do you know what this is? Do you care?

Geeks and their hobbies

The weird and wonderful world of geekdom is not limited to male members of the human race. It throws its shiny, chrome Starship Enterprise doors open with a satisfying 'swish' to anyone brave enough to want to venture within, and many women are more than happy to accept the invitation. But it is still a male-dominated world. What images do the words 'geek' and 'nerd' conjure up? A skinny, unhealthily pale creature, squinting out from behind glasses whose lenses are so thick they are probably bulletproof. He is wearing a white button-down shirt with a few leaky pens and what looks suspiciously like a calculator protruding from the pocket. He's forgotten to remove his bicycle clips from the legs of his high-waisted polyester trousers. Although he is well past school age, he wears a backpack, which is most likely stuffed to the brim with limited edition comics, Pokémon cards, leaflets for science-fiction conventions and Renaissance fairs and bits of computer hardware. Your mileage may vary, but whatever nightmarish vision wafted uninvited into your head, it was most definitely of the male variety.

Shameless stereotypes aside, many men indulge in hobbies that the rest of us dismiss, rightly or wrongly, as being completely and utterly 100 per cent geeky. We scoff, but they don't give a stuff, because the one thing all geeks have in common is their utter dedication and commitment to their chosen pastime, whatever it may be. So what are these hobbies that inspire so much devotion and obsession?

Science fiction and fantasy

'Your mouth says "Shields up" but your eyes say "A hull breach is imminent."'

'Somebody must have shot you with a phaser set on "stunning".'

'Tell me of this thing you humans call love.'

'Do you want to see what a true Jedi can do with his light sabre?'

'Earth woman, prepare to be probed.'

'Urkuk lu stalga.'

These chat-up lines favoured by science-fiction enthusiasts go a long way to explain why most of them find it virtually impossible to have any sort of liaison with a member of the opposite sex, as opposed to imaginary ones with female aliens on a mission to create a new human–alien race or Lieutenant Uhura from *Star Trek*. (That last one means 'I love you, baby' in Klingon, in case you were wondering.)

The most striking characteristic of true science-fiction and fantasy aficionados is their apparent inability to grasp the fact that most of it is, in fact, made up. They spend hours discussing the 'science' behind light sabres and holodecks and replicators and post long, unreadable articles about them on the Internet. A group of people with way too much time on their hands have actually invented the Elven language. Not just a few words and phrases, but an *entire language* with complex grammatical rules. There are people out there who actually believe that dragons exist. Where on earth they think these giant, fire-breathing creatures have been hanging out for millennia without being spotted, God only knows, but they are convinced that they are real. These people have clearly failed to spot where they are going wrong, although it is glaringly obvious to the rest of us: it is 'science fiction' not 'science fact' and 'fantasy' not 'reality'.

Also in the realms of the fantasy genre (though perhaps a bit more grounded in actual history than elves or dragons, albeit rather shaky history) are the Renaissance fairs. Or, more often, 'faires', because everyone knows that putting an 'e' on the ends of words instantly gives them that highly authentic olde-worlde feel. A good Renaissance fair can actually be quite fun, but there is something undeniably geeky about those middle-aged men who travel the length and breadth of the country in the summer months playing at being knights of the realm or squeezing their podgy legs into green nylon tights and pretending to be Robin Hood.

The minute you pay your entrance fee you'll be accosted by a man in a preposterous jester's outfit.

84

'Huzzah for the king!' he cries. 'Good morrow to you, mistress! A shilling for this fine tankard of mead!' Except it's not a shilling, is it? It's £1.50. And that's not a tankard of mead; it's a plastic cup filled with lukewarm lager. And then there's the 'jousting', which generally consists of two sweaty, red-faced men balanced precariously on bored-looking horses, ineffectually swiping at each other with padded sticks (unfortunately health and safety regulations do not allow jousts to the death with real weapons, more's the pity).

Video games

'I know I promised to mow the lawn this afternoon, honey, but I've just been given a mission to destroy the orcs that dwell in the Caves of Doom, and to do that I need to get my hands on the Magical Sword of Ultimate Power, which is going to take me a couple of hours at least because there's a group of trolls guarding it that I really don't like the look of and…OH MY GOD! Where did these ghouls come from!? They're all over me and I've run out of Sacred Potions of Healing! OH NO! I'M GOING TO DIE!'

No, you haven't just inadvertently wandered into a terrifying parallel universe and your man is not really in deadly peril. You are just unfortunate enough to be lumbered with a video game addict. There's not a lot you can do about the situation. You could pole-dance naked directly in his line of vision and he would still not be distracted from whatever improbable creature he is currently attempting to massacre. You could try investing in a Jordanesque boob job and donning a pair of hot pants and pretend to be Lara Croft, but it is unlikely to grab his attention, as hard-core gamers tend to prefer their women in pixelated form. Dressing up as a zombie or some other form of undead aberration is dangerous because he might suddenly attack you with his Ginormous Axe of Bloody Death.

No, the only solution is to join him in his obsession and spend day after day in a darkened room, bathed in the neon glow emanating from your TV screen or

 computer, your beloved by your side, united at last on your epic mission to rid a make-believe world

of evil monsters. You may lose your job, your house may slowly crumble around you, your kids may give themselves up to Social Services, but it will be worth it in the end, when you finally get your hands on the Elusive Armour of Unbeatable Superhuman Strength.

Money

Men are a bit funny when it comes to money. They think nothing about spending obscene amounts of cash buying useless bits of junk that they don't need and will never use (see Gadgets), but they stare at us in horror and disbelief when we occasionally splurge on the things that make us happy, like a new outfit or haircut. They visibly break out into a cold sweat when we announce we're off to do a bit of shopping.

'B-b-b-but what are you going to buy?' he stammers, a look of stricken terror on his face.

'Not much. I'm just going to do a bit of browsing and maybe buy a new pair of shoes.'

'More shoes!? Didn't you buy a new pair last year? What's wrong with the ones you've got on now?' He peers suspiciously at your feet. 'I don't see anything wrong with them!'

'Oh, for God's sake. It's not like I'm Carrie from

Sex and the City! It's just a pair of high-street shoes. They won't break the bank.'

'Well, don't go mad!'

This is why most sensible women apply the 10 per cent rule when showing their purchases to their partners, removing all the tags first and knocking at least 10 per cent off the actual price.

Men are also terrible hoarders, much worse than women. Like Wombles, they insist that they can make good use of the things that other people wouldn't hesitate to throw away. That towering pile of yellowing newspapers stashed in the attic, for example, might come in handy someday. Late one night there will be a frantic hammering at the door and a panic-stricken man will be standing there, pale as a ghost and gasping for breath. 'Quick!' he'll pant. 'It's a matter of life or death! I must know what was on page twenty of the *Sun* on the eighteenth of September, 1973. Please help me!' You just never know.

Of course this kind of behaviour is par for the course, typical of the male mentality. But some men take all this a step too far and make Ebenezer Scrooge look like the most beneficent philanthropist ever to walk the earth. So how can you tell whether you've been lumbered with a cheapskate? There are some pretty obvious clues.

❖ When you stay at a hotel, he steals all the little bottles of toiletries. No problem, you think, everyone does that. Then he produces several extra giant-sized holdalls from his suitcase and proceeds to strip the room of everything he is able to fit in them. Pillows, cushions, sheets, shower curtains, ashtrays, clock radios, lampshades, you name it – they all disappear into his magic Mary Poppins bags. It takes him several trips to lug them all to the car, right under the noses of the incredulous hotel staff.

❖ He is unable to walk past a skip without diving head-first into it and delving for hours among the filthy rubbish, while you stand red-faced on the pavement, forced to endure sympathetic looks from passers-by. Eventually he emerges, triumphantly clutching some grimy, smelly, flea-infested piece of crumbling furniture which he insists 'just needs a bit of spit and polish and it will be as good as new'.

❖ Dining out with him is a living hell. He'll only agree to such an extravagance under extreme duress, such as threats of imminent divorce proceedings. He takes his own cheese to McDonald's to avoid the 30p price difference between a hamburger and a cheeseburger. If by some miracle you manage to persuade him to take you to a real restaurant, he complains loudly about every dish, no matter how delicious, in the hope of getting a few pounds knocked off the bill. He asks for basket after basket of bread, which he then wraps up in napkins and hides in your handbag to take home. As for leaving a tip, forget about it. You can never go to the same restaurant more than once for fear that the waiters will remember you and spit in your food.

❖ Eating at home is not much better. He blags free fruit and vegetables in various states of decay at the local market, claiming they are for his non-existent rabbits. He makes 'tomato soup' out of sachets of ketchup from fast-food restaurants and hot water.

❖ Special occasions such as Valentine's Day and anniversaries are his idea of hell. Instead of buying you a card, he takes you to the card shop, picks out an appropriate one which he hands to you to read and then he puts it back on the shelf. The neighbours have given up on their previously lovingly tended gardens because any flowers they grew would mysteriously vanish from their beds in the middle of the night at certain times of the year.

Sport

There's nothing wrong with playing sports. It's a wonderful way to have fun, get some exercise, bond with your mates and learn how to be a valuable team player. The problem is that not many people actually participate in sports these days. Most of us haven't stepped onto a pitch since our schooldays, when we were forced to run pointlessly round an icy field in the depths of winter while some sadistic maniac of a P.E. teacher screamed abuse at us from the sidelines. After all, why bother to get all sweaty and red-faced and out of breath when you can watch someone else do all the hard work from the comfort of your sofa, a beer in one hand and a giant kebab in the other?

This is the problem with men who are obsessed with

sport. They don't do anything with their free time except watch other people running around or kicking balls or hitting each other, people who are only doing what they are doing because they are paid sickening amounts of money to do so, and these vast sums are only handed out because the sport-obsessed spectators are unwilling to get off their rotund backsides and go outside and get some exercise and fresh air and an actual life of their own. They talk the talk and walk the walk (or should that be waddle the waddle?), but they would rather gouge out their own eyeballs with a plastic fork than participate in any form of exercise themselves that is any more vigorous than a leisurely stroll to the chip shop.

There are certain times of the year that some of us dread. I'm talking about those of us who are not driven almost to the point of orgasm by watching a bunch of men kicking a ball (and often each other) round a pitch, or two people hitting a slightly smaller ball at each other over a net, or lots of men in white throwing a very hard ball at bits of wood. Unfortunately, these momentous sporting events usually coincide with the time of year when the birds are singing, the sun is shining and everyone should be outside enjoying the all-too-brief British summer. Instead, the streets are deserted and the birdsong is drowned out by the drunken roars of celebration or despair that emanate periodically from behind tightly closed and heavily curtained windows. If you are not a sports fan, then at times like this you are bang out of luck. All you can do is hang on in there and patiently wait for all the various tournaments to draw to their tedious conclusions.

Let's turn our attention to football at this point, because, after all, football is the national obsession. There is a lot to hate about football. The blanket coverage of the sport at almost any given time of the year means that there is no escape. And to admit to not caring how England fare in the international arena is akin to admitting to being a communist in 1950s America, or declaring that you think Osama Bin Laden is a jolly nice chap with some interesting ideas.

There is always some match on television, often on several channels simultaneously. One wonders how the football-loving male population would react if *Sleepless in Seattle* or *Bridget Jones's Diary* was broadcast on twenty channels on a continuous loop for several weeks at a time. Not very well, I'd wager. The newspapers aren't much better. No doubt if the world was about to come to an end, the public would be informed in tiny print squeezed in at the bottom of page two, following the earth-shattering news of the latest record-breaking transfer fee and David Beckham's new hairdo.

The tedious, inane and sometimes downright laughable commentary that accompanies televised matches does nothing to enhance the game, as shown by comments such as these:

'If history repeats itself, I should think we can expect the same thing again.' *Terry Venables*

'To play Holland, you have to play the Dutch.' *Ruud Gullit*

'For those of you watching in black and white, Spurs are in the all-yellow strip.' *John Motson*

'Strangely, in slow motion replay, the ball seemed to hang in the air for even longer.' *David Acfield*

'I would not say he is the best left-winger in the Premiership, but there are none better.' *Ron Atkinson*

'Yes, Woodcock would have scored, but his shot was just too perfect.' *Ron Atkinson*

'He dribbles a lot and the opposition don't like it – you can see it all over their faces.' *Ron Atkinson*. Again

'Well, either side could win it, or it could be a draw.' Yep, you guessed it. *Ron Atkinson*

'Beckenbauer has really gambled all his eggs.' *Guess who?*

⌇⌇⌇⌇⌇⌇⌇⌇⌇⌇⌇⌇⌇⌇⌇⌇⌇⌇⌇⌇⌇⌇⌇⌇

But even worse than having to listen to this rubbish is having to listen to the average man on the street talking about football. Not content with neglecting their families and going to every single match, or hogging the TV day in day out to watch their beloved team play, they have to talk about 'the beautiful game' for hour upon tedious hour. How can there possibly be so much to say? Two teams kick a ball around a pitch and try to get it to go in between two posts. One team wins, one team loses or they draw. End of. But no, on and on they blather, non-stop. And worse even than this is when they try to 'explain' some technicality of the game to a completely uninterested woman. Listen up, boys. It's not that our feeble female brains can't grasp the basics of the offside rule. It's not that complicated really. It's just that after a few seconds of your explanation, our eyes glaze over and we start thinking about what we're going to cook for dinner or what shade of paint we're going to use to redecorate the bedroom. A few more seconds and we lose the will to live entirely. So just stop trying to 'educate' us. We're not interested.

Professional football these days is nothing but a money making bandwagon. If your man is football crazy, the chances are that he spends more on his passion than he does on you. Not content with charging broadcasters millions of pounds to show games, the fat cats of the footballing world cynically exploit the sheep-like mentality of hard-core fans to make even more money, charging a small fortune for season tickets and changing strips every few minutes, all the while rubbing their hands with glee and pouring bottles of Krug and fistfuls of caviar down their necks in their air-conditioned boardrooms. Meanwhile, a constant parade of moronic footballers appear on our screens and in our newspapers whingeing that their ludicrously inflated salaries are just not enough to keep them in Ferraris or their equally moronic WAGS kitted out from head to foot in Burberry.

So, who do you think is going to win the league this season? The red team or the blue team?

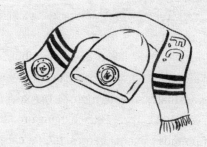

Bad Habits

Things That Make You Go Eww'

Let's be fair here (for a little while at least): male or female, we all have bad habits, whether it be nose-picking, nail-biting or knuckle-cracking. Women, however, tend to be more self-aware when it comes to their less-than-savoury practices. They might indulge in a lengthy nose-picking session once in a while (let's face it, it is a singularly satisfying experience), but they will usually be somewhat discreet about it, generally saving this enjoyable pastime for when they are in the privacy of their own home, behind closed doors, with no one around to witness it. Men, on the other hand, seem to be blissfully unaware that they are indulging in habits so revolting that they would be thrown into jail if they lived in a less tolerant society. Either that or they just don't care. Disgusting personal practices seem to be a hot topic among women who love to moan about men, so let's take a quick look at some of the most prevalent.

WARNING: The following descriptions may cause nausea, vomiting and severe trauma. Read on at your own peril.

Farting

Men have found the act of passing wind to be hilarious since the moment one of the first cavemen turned to his companion round the campfire and said, 'Oi, Dave, pull my finger.' Trumping, fluffing, parping, guffing, letting rip, blowing off, passing gas, peeling the paint off the walls, cutting the cheese, fog-horning, flutter-blasting, expelling the ghosts of long-dead beans – whatever you want to call it, men have been laughing about it, talking about it and positively revelling in it since the beginning of time, and will still be doing so at the bitter end, when the earth finally explodes in a methane-fuelled ball of fire.

They are biologically wired this way and no amount of nagging will convince them that it is not polite to let rip whenever they feel the urge. They look at you with wide-eyed, outraged innocence when you dare to express your disgust at the foul stench which has just assaulted your nostrils, claiming, 'Better out than in!' Is it? Is it really? Better for whom? Certainly not for me, or anyone else within a two-mile radius. Don't be fooled by all this talk of 'It's natural!' or 'It's not healthy to hold it in!' There's nothing natural or healthy about the unholy stench men can seemingly endlessly produce. They don't do it because they genuinely believe that we should all be less hung up about our natural bodily functions. They do it because they know we hate it and because they find it funny.

The louder and smellier the fart, the better, and if they manage to embarrass you in a public place, then that is just the icing on the cake. There is nothing funnier, in their tiny minds, than letting one off in the middle of Sainsbury's on a busy Saturday morning and then legging it up the aisle, leaving you standing there, red in the face and looking guilty as hell, forced to endure the disgusted glares of fellow shoppers.

They love to talk about all things fart-related amongst themselves and, better still, compete with each other as to who can do the loudest, smelliest, longest, most amusing etc. fart. It has become a form of communication amongst the male species, their own special language – like the one used by dolphins. Men who can fart on demand are revered by their peers. Take Le Pétomane, farter extraordinaire, who took Paris by storm in the 1890s with his trump-filled stage show which included a rendition of the Marseillaise played by an orchestra of one – his bum. Men flocked to his show in their hundreds, prince and pauper alike, and he became the highest-paid performer of his generation. Audiences became so over-come with hysterical laughter, apparently, that trained nurses had to be hired by the theatre to be on standby with smelling salts.

It is hard for us women to understand this particular male obsession, so in the interests of research here are a few favourite fart sayings and stories, told by men in their own words. Who knows, it might help us be more tolerant and more understanding of this favourite pastime of the average British male. It might, but it probably won't.

∽∾∽∾∽∾∽∾∽∾∽∾∽∾∽∾∽∾∽∾∽∾∽

'Wherever you be, let the wind blow free.
Be it church or chapel, let the bugger rattle.'

'The reason farts smell is so that deaf people can enjoy them too.'

'If someone lets off a fruity whiff, it is impolite and an opportunity missed if you don't pass on your opinions to the owner.'

'I managed to light one the other day. I felt a real sense of achievement as I had never succeeded before. I felt very fulfilled.'

'When I let out a particularly offensive trump in the car, I override the electric windows, so my passengers are forced to fully appreciate it.'

'My girlfriend complains when I fart on her in bed, but it's just my way of saying "I love you." Plus, it's a cheaper way of keeping warm than keeping the central heating on at night.'

'I was forced to go shopping for bedlinen with my wife and I was bored out of my mind. I grabbed a vase from one of the shelves, farted in it and passed it to her, saying, "Does this vase smell funny to you?" The look on her face when she caught a whiff of it was priceless!'

'My dog is so fed up with me farting on him that

he now growls if anyone's bum comes anywhere near him.'

'Fart-throwing is a favourite hobby in my house. Grab a handful as it comes out, then fling it in the direction of the nearest person. If you really want to go to town, though, fart in a jam jar, screw the lid back on, leave it for a week, then release it under the nose of your victim. It is horrific!'

∽∽∽∽∽∽∽∽∽∽∽∽∽∽∽∽∽∽∽∽∽∽∽∽∽

Nose-picking

How many times have you been stuck in traffic and have innocently glanced into an adjoining car only to be assaulted by the delightful sight of a man with one finger thrust up to the knuckle in his nostril, happily digging away as if he were mining for gold? There is a horrible fascination in watching this process take place. The gentleman in question usually has a blissed-out, slightly glazed look in his eyes, as if he were receiving a deep-muscle massage or some other equally soothing treatment in a high-end spa. You find you can't tear your eyes away as you wonder what he will do with the fruits of his labour. It is unlikely that there will be a tissue involved in the process, so where will it go? More often than not, his hand will eventually disappear from view, to be wiped clean on a trouser leg or some secret spot within the car itself, where no doubt there is already an impressive collection of bogies eagerly waiting to greet the new addition. But if you are really unlucky, you might see the finger slowly emerge and – oh, God no! – inch its way down towards the mouth. At this point you will no doubt be bitterly regretting your act of voyeurism and praying for the lights to change, so that you can move on with your life and try to put the trauma behind you. Many men don't see anything wrong with this nauseating practice (as one gentleman put it: 'I think it's just insane to waste something that my body has spent so long building up. It's legitimate protein, after all'), but we know that it is wrong. Oh so very wrong.

Toenail clippings

Some men form strong attachments to body parts which the rest of us wouldn't think twice about disposing of. This is especially true of toenail clippings. They can't bear to throw them away. They leave little piles of them, like memorial cairns, on the side of the bath and a liberal sprinkling of yellowing, razor-sharp shards all over the living-room carpet. Some men have even raised the humble toenail clipping to art form, with one artist displaying five years' worth of clippings in a glass dome and another creating a collage which, according to critics, 'playfully explores issues of self, ego and identity'.

The rearranging of private parts

Jiggle, jiggle, jiggle, prod, prod, prod, scratch, scratch, scratch. All day long. Why the constant need to touch themselves 'down there'? Is it to reassure themselves that it is still there, that it hasn't packed its bags and gone off to find a cleaner, more hygienic abode? Do they think it will fall off if they don't hold it in place? Are they so proud of their endowments that they wish to draw attention to them, making women swoon and other men green with envy at the sight of their mighty loins? Will we ever learn the answers to these questions?

Spitting

In the Middle Ages, spitting was commonplace and socially acceptable. It was perfectly all right to stop mid-conversation in order to hawk up a nice juicy mouthful of phlegm and spray it at the feet of whomever it was that you were talking to, be they pauper or royalty. Fortunately for those of us whose stomachs turn at the sight of such a revolting practice, this is no longer the case. So why is it that some men still cannot grasp the fact that spitting in public is the height of rudeness? Why must we still put up with that horribly ominous snotty noise, which sounds like someone is trying to suck their brains out and which warns us to duck for cover lest we be hit by a ball of phlegm travelling at the speed of light? Do they really want to revert back to the good old days of the Middle Ages? Perhaps we should remind them of some of the other customs of the time, which they may not find so appealing, such as the fact that it was only acceptable to make love to your wife if it wasn't Lent, Advent, Whitsun week, Easter week, a feast day, a fast day, a Sunday, a Wednesday, a Friday or a Saturday.

Lying

Women lie to men. Men lie to women. We all do it, be it a little white fib or the occasional shameless porky of such mammoth proportions that we can almost feel our noses expanding out from our faces at an alarming rate. But studies have shown that men and women tend to lie for different reasons. Women are more prone to white lies, told to make someone feel better or to avoid hurt feelings ('You're much better-looking than Johnny Depp. I don't fancy him at all' or 'No, the dinner you cooked was delicious. I must have caught a stomach bug from someone at work' or 'I really love the orange and purple crocheted top you bought me for Christmas. It's too nice to wear every day so I'm saving it for a special occasion.') Men, on the other hand, tend to lie for two reasons: to protect their fragile egos and to get themselves out of trouble.

It is the 'getting out of hot water' lies that we are most concerned with here, rather than the ego-boosting ones. After all, if you've been with a guy for longer than two minutes, you will have sussed out that he is in fact a plumber and not a 'lavatorial engineering specialist' and that he may indeed have gone to Oxford, but only once, on a stag night. He'll have stopped telling you these sorts of silly lies the minute he hoodwinked you into starting some sort of relationship with him. The other kinds of lies though, the pathetic excuses he comes up with when he knows he's in trouble, never end.

The saddest thing about the lying men do is that they are so crap at it. Women are expert liars. Men are incompetent amateurs. But their egos do not allow them to admit this to themselves, which is why they express such astonishment at the amazing powers of 'intuition' that we women supposedly have when it comes to sniffing out their feeble fibs. Of course the reality is that even the most gullible child, one who still believes in Father Christmas and the Tooth Fairy, would see right through him.

Many of these lies are brought about by a condition that most men suffer from. Manesia is a very specific type of forgetfulness. Men have no problem remembering who scored the goal in the seventh minute of the 1982 FA Cup final and other useless bits of trivia, but they struggle to remember their own wedding anniversaries, the birthdays of their loved ones and other special occasions, despite the fact that these events all occur every year, on the exact same day. It's one thing to forget someone's birthday or your wedding anniversary – unforgivable, but understandable given their limited powers of recollection – but it's quite mind-boggling how many men manage to forget Valentine's Day, given that, in these times of frenzied commercialism and consumerism, everywhere you look for days beforehand you see hearts and roses and boxes of chocolates and bottles of pink champagne. It's almost like forgetting Christmas. But forget they do and then out pour the lies and excuses, as they try to weasel their way out of the situation they have brought upon themselves.

'You never age in my eyes. That's why I always forget your birthday.' This kind of shamelessly cynical flattery is bad enough. Worse is the flat-out denial. 'I didn't forget! I ordered your present weeks ago! It's the company's fault for not delivering it on time. I'll call them and give them a piece of my mind.'

'Go on then,' you say.

'Um, I'll do it later. They'll all be on their lunch break now.'

'It's half-ten in the morning. Call them now.' And you settle down on the sofa, half angry, half amused, to watch as he shouts down the phone at some poor bemused employee who has no idea what he is talking about.

The deny-all-knowledge tactic is one often employed by small children and grown men alike. It's one thing to catch your six year old red-handed, sitting next to a graffitied stretch of wall, surrounded by crayons, and be told that the culprit was a six-foot orange dragon who flew in through the window, did the deed and flew back out again. It is somewhat less amusing and endearing when your adult partner spins you an equally fantastical tale to explain some wrongdoing.

'I know I was supposed to pick you up at your sister's house. What happened was that I was all ready to leave and I dropped the car keys down the toilet and my hand got stuck trying to fish them out, and it took me ages to pull it out. Then as I was driving down the high street, there was this pregnant woman who needed a lift to the hospital and there were no taxis, so I said I'd take her, but she went into premature labour in the back seat and I had to pull over and deliver the baby myself. Then, as I was finally on my way over, I got stuck in a horrendous traffic jam caused by a herd of elephants that had escaped from the zoo and they kept charging at the car, so I thought it would be best just to turn around and go back home. And that's why I didn't turn up.'

It's not just their partners who have to put up with these tales of woe that stretch the bounds of credulity. They do it when it comes to skiving off work too. Women know to keep things simple when pulling a sickie. 'I have flu' is sufficient. Men over-elaborate and get caught out because they forget what they said (manesia again). 'I have flu AND my dog bit me on the ankle AND my grandmother died AND the car wouldn't start AND I got abducted by aliens…' Too much information, very little credibility. They can't seem to grasp the basic rules of the fine art of simple and effective fibbing, as shown by this collection of real-life excuses given by men to their incredulous bosses to explain their absence from work.

* While rowing across the river to work, I got lost in the fog.
* Someone stole all my daffodils.

- I have transient amnesia and couldn't remember my job.
- I accidentally drove through the automatic garage door before it opened.
- The ghosts in my house kept me up all night.
- I forgot I was getting married today. [This one could well be true.]
- My cow bit me.
- My son accidentally fell asleep next to wet cement in our garden. His foot fell in and we can't get it out.
- I wasn't thinking and accidentally went to my old job.
- I was arrested as a result of mistaken identity.
- I couldn't find my shoes.
- A hitman was looking for me.
- My cat unplugged my alarm clock.
- My monkey died.

Laziness

Isn't it amazing how men are able to sit around doing nothing for extended periods of time? Most women will sit down with a cup of tea and a magazine and instantly start to feel guilty about something or other. The mound of ironing of Mount Everest proportions, the teetering pile of dirty dishes in the sink, the grimy kitchen floor – all these things seem to take on a life of their own, glaring at you accusingly from their various positions in the house as if to say, 'How dare you sit around reading about some minor celebrity's wedding when there's work to be done! Come and deal with me RIGHT NOW, you lazy moo!' The average male, though, once he is comfortably ensconced on the sofa, is likely to remain there for the rest of the day, as if superglued to the cushions, only vacating his seat in dire circumstances, such as an approaching tsunami or if he needs to get

himself another beer. This is perhaps a throwback to prehistoric times, when men had to remain as still as possible in order to effectively hunt for prey. The fidgeters would be instantly gobbled up by a sabre-toothed tiger, thus ensuring that only those who had perfected the fine art of doing absolutely nothing survived to pass on their genes to their male descendants. A sad state of affairs for the modern woman.

This behaviour is not limited to the human species. Take lions for example. The lioness spends the majority of her time hunting for food for her family. What does the male lion do all day? Apart from a spot of sunbathing, bugger all. She's rushing around in the blazing heat trying to bring down an antelope or two, while he's stretched out on his nice warm rock, watching proceedings with a half-hearted, idle curiosity, probably giving her a few bits of unwanted and unhelpful advice. 'No, no, you don't want to do it like that. He's getting away! Come at him from the left a bit. That's it. You nearly got him that time. For God's sake, put a bit of effort into it, woman! I'll come and help you in a bit, just as soon as I've had my afternoon nap....'

The ability of the lion to spend 90 per cent of his life asleep given half the chance is shared by human males also. It is quite extraordinary, and enviable, how men are able to fall sleep anywhere, anytime, no matter how noisy or uncomfortable his surroundings are. He'll sit down on one of those hard, plastic, excruciatingly uncomfortable airport chairs – clearly invented by a sadist who bitterly hates his fellow human beings and wishes to inflict as much pain on them as possible – and he'll instantly fall asleep, despite the hordes of screaming children surrounding him and the deafening tannoy announcements every couple of seconds. Of course, he'll then indignantly and adamantly deny that he was snoozing, as if you were accusing him of some dreadful crime. 'I was NOT asleep! I was merely resting my eyes!' It's funny how so many men have 'tired eyes' syndrome. They really should see an optician about it.

This inherent laziness is the main cause of one of the most common of male sins: procrastination. 'Never put off until tomorrow what you can do the day after tomorrow,' said Mark Twain, a mantra that has been enthusiastically taken up by men ever since. The world is full of unfinished jobs – half-painted walls, semi-constructed shelves, not-quite-mended toasters. They start off with such good intentions, industriously lining up their paint pots and cleaning their brushes, bursting with pride at how efficient they are being. But after a few minutes they start to lose interest and run out of steam.

They suddenly remember another chore they promised you they would do many moons ago. 'I'd better go and do that first,' they think. 'It's a more pressing job.' 'More pressing' meaning that it requires less effort. And so off they wander to start but not finish yet another project, telling themselves, 'I'll finish this some other day.' The problem is, of course, that Someotherday is not actually a day of the week.

Snoring

It's a common scenario. There you are, deep in a blissful slumber. You are having a lovely dream that you are lying by the side of a beautiful swimming pool. The tropical sun beats down on you and a gentle breeze stirs the branches of the palm trees. George Clooney is there, gently rubbing sun cream onto your shoulders. You can see Brad Pitt approaching, wearing nowt but a rather fetching pair of tight swimming trunks and carrying a tray on which rests a delicious-looking cocktail. It's even got a little paper umbrella in it. He reaches your side, smiles down at you and opens his mouth to say something.

'HCHCHCHCHCH-PFTPFTPFTPFT-HCHCHCHCHC-PFTPFTPFTPFT.'

'What the hell was that?! Brad, are you OK?'

And then you open your eyes and reality cruelly reasserts itself. There's no swimming pool, no palm trees, no cocktail, and the man lying beside you making that unearthly racket is most definitely not Brad Pitt.

You lie there for a while, listening to the horrible noise. It sounds like a freight train is passing through your bedroom at top speed. Maybe he'll stop in a minute. But no, five or ten minutes pass and the snoring shows no sign of abating. In fact, it seems to be getting worse. You prod him sharply in the ribs. He mumbles something and swats at your hand in his sleep, but he doesn't wake up. You poke him again, much harder this time. He'll have a nasty bruise in the morning, but still he slumbers on. In desperation, you kick him viciously in the shin. Victory! He's stopped!

You settle down and are just drifting back to sleep, hoping you'll be transported straight back to the pool and Brad Pitt, when suddenly: 'HCHCHCHCHCH-PFTPFTPFTPFT-HCHCHCHCHC-PFTPFTPFTPFT.'

You press a pillow over your head. The noise is slightly muffled, but you can still hear it. It's no longer a freight train now; it's more like an angry warthog. You consider pressing a pillow over his head, until he stops breathing altogether. Surely that would be justifiable homicide?

No jury would convict you, you think, and if they did, at least you would get a decent night's kip in your nice quiet cell. But you decide that this is probably taking things a bit too far. You need to either wake him up or get him to turn onto his side.

You reach over and grab a glass of water from your bedside table. You carefully position it over his head and dribble a bit onto his face. He splutters and snorts, but shows no signs of waking. You place your hands on his shoulder and push with all your might, but he is a dead weight, seemingly superglued to the mattress. You get out of bed and move over to his side. You grab his arm and try to tug him onto his side. You nearly pull it out of its socket, but he doesn't move an inch. How can he possibly sleep through all this physical abuse?

It's time to admit defeat. You grab a pillow and resign yourself to spending a lonely, uncomfortable night on the lumpy sofabed in the spare room. The next morning you are in the kitchen, bleary-eyed, muscles aching, when he comes bouncing in, all bright-eyed and bushy-tailed.

'Sleep well?' you ask, your voice dripping with sarcasm.

'No,' he says, giving you a pitiful look. 'I couldn't sleep. I was up all night.'

Tactlessness

There's an old military joke that goes something like this:

The captain calls the sergeant into his office one day and says, 'Sarge, I've just received a telegram informing me that Private Green's mother died. Please break the news to him and tell him to come and see me.'

The sergeant goes off to conduct the morning inspection of his troops and give out orders. 'Listen up, men,' he says. 'Peters, report to the mess hall. Jones, report to personnel. The rest of you report to the artillery officer. Oh and by the way, Green, your mother is dead. Report to the captain.'

Later that day, the captain calls the sergeant back to his office. 'Look, Sarge, that was a pretty cold way to break the news to poor Private Green. Try to be a bit more tactful next time, would you?'

'No problem, sir,' says the sergeant.

A few months later, the captain receives a telegram. This time, Private Smith's mother has died. Again, he asks his sergeant to break the news, reminding him to employ a bit more tact.

The sergeant lines his troops up for inspection.

'OK, listen up, men. I want everyone who has a
mother to take a step forward. NOT SO FAST,
SMITH!'

It doesn't take a genius to figure out the right thing to say
when you are in a bit of a sensitive situation. It's not
rocket science. So why is it that men often say exactly
the wrong thing at exactly the wrong time?

Take the age-old question which men the world over
dread hearing from the lips of their beloved wives and
girlfriends: 'Does my bum look big in this?' The correct
answer to this question is not, 'Yes, it looks absolutely
enormous, like two pigs fighting under a blanket.' Nor is
it, 'A bit.' Of course, no man in his right mind would dare
to utter either of these two replies, unless he had some
sort of death wish, but they do seem to find it
inordinately difficult to come up with the correct answer,
which is, 'No, you look absolutely fantastic in that outfit.'
What we usually get is something like this:

'Umm, what? Er, I dunno, whatever *you* think. You
have pretty eyes. Oh, look, there's a squirrel in the tree
outside the window. Oops, I think I might have left the
hob on. Must go and check.' And off they run before they
get themselves into any more trouble. Why can't they
just say, 'Your bum looks tiny, positively minute. You

could fit it into a pint glass'? Yes, it may well be a lie, but it is a good lie, a tactful lie. They can't seem to get their heads round this.

'We don't know what you want us to say!' they wail. 'When we lie to you, you shout at us and make us sleep in the spare room and tell us not to do it again. But then when we tell you the truth you shout at us and make us sleep in the spare room and tell us not to do it again. What do you want from us? We're so confused!'

But it's not really that confusing is it, boys? We want you to tell us the truth about where you were all night or why there's a dent the size of Denmark on the side of the car, but when it comes to the proportions of our backsides or other such issues, it's OK to fib a little. In fact, it is compulsory.

It's not just when it comes to answering questions that men are lacking in the tact department. Their own questioning techniques leave a lot to be desired. Any woman who works from home or is a stay-at-home mum or housewife has heard the dreaded 'What have you done all day?' at one time (after the first time, they usually have the sense never to ask again). Of course, what they generally mean by this is 'Did you have a good day?', but this is not what comes out of their mouths and the inference that we have sat around all day doing bugger all instantly makes us go on the defensive.

'Oh, well, let me see. I spent most of the morning on the couch watching daytime TV while the kids washed and dressed themselves. Then I lay in the bath for a few hours with a book while the servants made the beds, mopped the kitchen floor, vacuumed the living room and did all the washing and ironing. I was knackered by then, so I had a bit of a nap and then Johnny Depp came round for lunch and we had a lovely time playing Pirate and Wench and Hide the Cannon. After that I had tea and crumpets at the Ritz before rushing home just in time to watch *Countdown*.'

Looking Good, Feeling Good

Fashion

If the media are to be believed, the last decade or so has seen a revolution in men's fashion. Apparently, these days heterosexual men are just as obsessed with fashion and grooming as women and gay men, and the sheer volume of men's fashion magazines and grooming products available on the market would suggest that this is true. But where are these stylish, perfectly groomed straight men? Do you know any? Do you see any of these mythical George Clooney lookalikes strolling down the high street on an average Saturday afternoon? After years of just throwing on whatever garment is not so filthy that it has grown legs and slunk away or meekly wearing whatever their wives or mothers buy for them, men are simply bewildered by the endless, often conflicting fashion advice being thrown at them. With this in mind, here are a few simple-to-follow top tips for the poor style-challenged creatures.

Sportswear

Yes, tracksuits are comfortable. But so is slobbing around the house all day in your dressing gown and you wouldn't be seen out on the streets in it (if you would, please stop reading this now – you are beyond any help). Unless you are actually going to the gym or for a run or to play football in the park, leave the tracksuit at home where it belongs. Perhaps this is a tad unfair, but it is hard to believe that the men most often seen wearing sporty ensembles, their double chins wobbling and beer guts merrily jiggling as they waddle down the street, are in training for anything other than the Annual Pie-eating Championships.

Sandals with socks

It's shocking that this old chestnut must be brought up in this day and age, after so many years of brutal but fully deserved scorn and mickey-taking. Men, why can't you get to grips with the fact that the sandals-and-socks combo makes you look like utter gits? Why do you insist on committing this particular fashion crime over and over? Is it just to annoy us? Because there can't be any other good reason. Isn't the point of wearing a pair of sandals to keep your feet cool in the summer? Therefore it stands to reason, does it not, that adding a pair of socks totally defeats the purpose. If it's too cold to bare your feet, wear a pair of shoes!

High-rise or low-rise

Judging by the walking, talking fashion disasters we see every day, it seems that finding a decent pair of men's trousers that actually fit is a virtually impossible task akin to one of the twelve labours of Hercules. Surely it can't be that hard to find a pair of trousers that a) don't expose the full glory of your hairy bum cleavage to unsuspecting passers-by or b) have to be tightly belted just under your armpits, in the style made so infamous by the sartorially challenged Simon

Cowell before he came to his senses. There must be a middle ground. Please find it.

In other trouser-related madness, why are teenage boys still wearing those trousers with crotches that come down to their knees, at the same time exposing a good few inches of their grimy boxer shorts? This is one crime that makes you yearn for a panic button that is directly linked to the fashion police headquarters. You are torn between pity and hysterical laughter at the sight of those already awkward adolescents walking with that ridiculous wide-legged swagger which is the only thing preventing their trousers from falling down around their ankles. Still, this is preferable to the latest teenage fashion of wearing tracksuit bottoms with one leg pulled up to just below the knee. What on earth is this all about?

Toupees

Most men are genetically predisposed to hair loss. This is, of course, a bit of a bummer for you, but it really isn't that big a deal. Why not take comfort from the fact that you are in good company – with over 70 per cent of men experiencing male-pattern baldness sooner or later – instead of obsessing about your locks (or lack thereof)? Why won't you believe us when we tell you that bald men are sexier than men in toupees? We are not lying. Take a look at men like Bruce Willis, Patrick Stewart and Ed Harris and then picture them with dead cats perched precariously on their heads. Would they look more virile? More masculine? More appealing? No, they would not. They would look like prats. A toupee is still better than a comb-over though. Anything is better than a comb-over.

Speedos

Unless you have the body of an Adonis, Speedos are not a good look. We cannot stress this enough. Even if you do have a body to rival that of Michaelangelo's 'David', nobody wants to see your bits in such graphic detail, believe us. And don't forget that no matter how well endowed you are, a dip in cold water means instant shrinkage. If this isn't enough to put you off, just remember that Tony Blair likes to wear them when he is on holiday.

Cardigans

Just because Jude Law and David Beckham have been seen sporting cardigans, doesn't mean you should. There is a difference between a trendy Paul Smith number and that grey, misshapen rag with egg-yolk stains down the front that you misguidedly call an item of clothing.

Illness

A man lies on the sofa, his eyes half closed, his hand resting on his clammy brow, in an attitude that suggests great suffering and unimaginable pain. Every sneeze and cough is accompanied by a tortured groan. Every time he reaches for a tissue, he winces and groans some more, as if someone had just prodded him with a red-hot poker. He is surrounded by dozens of pill bottles, packets and nasal sprays – enough to enable him to open his own pharmacy. He reaches out a trembling hand, but is too weak to grasp the steaming mug of Lemsip beside him.

'Sweetheart?' he croaks feebly, in little more than a whisper. There is no reply.

'Sweetheart, please.' He raises his voice a little this time, but the effort causes him to clutch at his head and moan softly.

A harassed-looking woman appears in the doorway. 'What is it? What's wrong?' There is a long pause, punctuated only by the soft moaning noise he is still making. Eventually it subsides.

'I'm…not…feeling…very…good.'

'I know. Is there anything I can do for you?'

'No, nothing can be done,' he whispers. 'I'm…dying.'

This pathetic creature is suffering from one of the worst, most virulent diseases man has ever known. The spread of this disease is unstoppable; it is an epidemic of mammoth proportions. In a cruel twist of fate, only the male of the species can contract it, although it can be carried and spread by women in the form of a non-life-threatening cold. This disease is, of course, Man Flu and it is not to be sniffed at, if you'll pardon the pun. Unfortunately, there is no known cure.

Man Flu is a reality, says a survey conducted by *Nuts* magazine. Two-thirds of British men suffer from Man Flu come the winter months and it is responsible for 30 million lost work days every year. Men take an average of three days to recover from a cold compared to one and a half days for women, with 82 per cent of the men surveyed saying they took to their beds, while 66 per cent of women went about their business as normal. The *Nuts* health correspondent sent up this impassioned plea: 'Our womenfolk must go that extra mile to care for us when we are stricken. That way cars can be maintained and football stadia throughout the land can be well attended.'

So there you have it, ladies, look after your men when they are ill or else the world as we know it will come to an end. It is seemingly impossible for a man suffering from Man Flu to grasp the fact that the mild cold his girlfriend had the week before and his own debilitating illness must be one and the same. 'There is no way,' he thinks to himself, 'that I have what she had. She got up, went to work, picked up the kids, cooked dinner and tidied up after us all and I can only lie here shivering under my duvet for days on end. There's something seriously wrong with me. Maybe I should call an ambulance.'

Studies have shown that men and women suffer from hypochondria equally. This is no doubt true, but while in general hypochondria in women manifests itself as a mild form of neurosis, male sufferers throw themselves into it with all the zest and zeal of one who has discovered a new, endlessly fascinating hobby. They'll invest in one of those huge medical dictionaries and spend hours poring over it, anxiously checking to see if they have any symptoms and then self-diagnosing all sorts of terrifying, life-threatening illnesses. A mild case of indigestion becomes the first signs of a massive heart attack. A few trips to the loo during the night is a sure sign of prostate cancer, with no thought being given to the five pints of lager they consumed before they went to bed.

Ironically, given the song and dance men like to make about their minor complaints, they will only go to see a doctor if they are actually at death's door, having coughed up a lung or something, and even then they will only book an appointment under extreme duress and after many hours of trying to get out of it. ('What lung? Oh, *this* lung. Stop making such a fuss, woman. I'll just stuff it back in, no need to bother the doctor with such a trivial thing.')

This is actually a major healthcare issue and one that has prompted much debate. The Men's Health Forum conducted a survey a few years ago asking men what it would take to get them to visit the doctor more often. The results were depressingly predictable. Many complained that surgeries were too girly in terms of decor. Presumably they mean that they are usually clean and tidy and furnished with comfortable chairs rather than sticky, beer-soaked carpets and bar stools. One man suggested showing old cowboy films and another televised football. An excellent idea, boys, because of course the sounds of gunfire and roaring, chanting crowds is exactly what you want when you are poorly. One poor deluded soul simply begged: 'Be less formal; make it more fun.' And one man took the whole thing way too far and suggested that surgeries be held in more man-friendly environments, such as betting shops, pubs and golf clubs. Good grief. Has it really come to this?

Mid-life Crisis

We all look back on the glorious, golden days of our youth with a kind of misty-eyed nostalgia. We all sometimes long for a return to the days when we were footloose and fancy-free, when we had nothing to worry about other than scraping through the odd exam and whether that certain someone we've had our eye on is interested or just hanging around because they fancy our best mate. But for most of us, these occasional forays into the realm of fantasy remain just that: bittersweet daydreams.

But something happens to some men when they reach a certain age. They'll wake up one morning, haul themselves out of bed and into the bathroom, glance in the mirror and then freeze as a terrible realisation starts to slowly creep over them. They'll stare in horror at the wrinkles, receding hairline and beer gut, as if seeing them for the first time. 'What's happened to me? People used to tell me I was a dead ringer for David Cassidy; now I look like David Mellor. Oh God, this can't be right. There's something wrong with the mirror.'

They'll go about the rest of the day in a horrified trance, becoming more and more depressed as they contemplate the reality of their middle-aged lives, lives which they had hitherto been perfectly contented and at peace with. Suddenly, their decently paid jobs, their long-suffering, tolerant wives and their loving if sometimes troublesome teenage children seem like nothing more than yokes around their necks. Their ears ring with the sounds of doors clanging shut and keys being turned in locks behind them as they are marched with alarming speed down the prison corridors of their remaining years of life, towards the terrible inevitability of old age and death. 'Oh no. No siree. I will not let this happen. I will break free. I will recapture some of my lost youth before it is too late.' This is when the trouble begins.

Women living with men going through a mid-life crisis are women living life on the edge. It can be exhilarating, nerve-wracking, horrifying, devastating, embarrassing or hilarious, or all of these at once. You just don't know what form the metamorphosis is going to take. All you can do is sit helplessly on the sidelines and hope that when it all blows over, the dust settles and some semblance of normality starts to creep back in, your life won't be turned upside-down, or at least not irreparably so. The male mid-life crisis, the man-o-pause if you will, can take many forms. Let's take a whirlwind tour through some of the most common.

Getting down with the kids

This particular form of crisis can be firmly placed in the 'embarrassing' category. The man who previously used to sit around all day in his cardigan and slippers reading the *Guardian*, moaning about how 'the youth of today have no respect for their elders' and shouting at the kids to 'turn that bloody awful racket down' will suddenly transform into a grotesque parody of a hip teenager, throwing himself wholeheartedly into all things to do with youth culture.

∽∽ ∽∽ ∽∽ ∽∽ ∽∽ ∽∽ ∽∽ ∽∽ ∽∽ ∽∽

The signs

❖ He peppers his conversations with words like
  'dude' and 'awesome' ('Like, dude, the new
  Green Day album is, like, totally awesome!').

❖ Instead of ringing you, he texts (IM WRKNG
  L8 TNGHT. BCK IN TM FR DNNR).

❖ He starts calling you 'babe'.

❖ He sets up a profile on MySpace.

❖ He stays up all night killing zombies on the
  PlayStation.

❖ He swaps your annual holiday in Tuscany for
  a two-week rave-up in Ibiza.

∽∽ ∽∽ ∽∽ ∽∽ ∽∽ ∽∽ ∽∽ ∽∽ ∽∽ ∽∽

Easy Rider

For some men, the approach of middle age brings with
it an irresistible urge to get the motor running and head
out on the highway, even if the closest they've ever come
to succumbing to the lure of the open road before is the
annual caravanning holiday in the Lake District. You'll
come home one day to find the family Volvo Estate
conspicuously absent. In its place will be a monstrosity
of a motorbike, covered from top to bottom with chrome

and menacing painted-on flames. 'Oh no!' you'll think. 'Have we been burgled by a gang of bikers?' You'll cautiously open the front door and retreat in alarm as a sinister figure dressed in black leather and wearing a helmet with a tinted visor appears in the living-room doorway. 'Please don't hurt me,' you'll whimper. 'Take what you want and go…' and then you'll stop in your tracks as the helmet is removed to reveal the sheepishly grinning face of your own dearly beloved.

The signs

❖ He gives himself a biker-style nickname, like 'Flash Fred' or 'Hound Dawg Doug'.

❖ He insists on wearing leather from head to toe, no matter where he is going or how hot it is.

❖ He gets a full-body tattoo, involving images of skulls, naked women, motorbikes or naked women on motorbikes with skulls instead of faces.

❖ He insists on growing a sad, scraggly little grey ponytail and says he will divorce you if you carry out one of your numerous threats to cut it off while he is asleep.

Vanity, thy name is man

Your man has had the same pair of jeans for twenty years. Despite the fact that they have partially disintegrated over the years, particularly around the crotch area, until only a single, fraying thread is saving him from public shame, he insists that they have plenty of wear left in them and refuses to replace them because they are comfortable and that is all he cares about. His idea of personal grooming is a quick shower (no need to scrub or anything because 'the water runs down and washes the dirt away by itself') and a cursory swipe with a comb somewhere in the vicinity of his head. He clips his nails with his teeth. His idea of a workout is a leisurely stroll to the nearest Chinese takeaway.

But, suddenly, overnight, all this changes. Faced with the grim realities of the changes wrought by time on the human body, this same man has been transformed into a creature so obsessed with his appearance that he would put the average, twenty-something male model to shame.

The signs

❖ You can't get into the bathroom for love nor money as he is barricaded in there night and day, preening, tweezing, waxing and exfoliating.

❖ He constantly asks you, 'Does my bum look big in this?'

❖ He goes away 'on a business trip' and returns with a new nose/full head of hair/wrinkle-free complexion.

Men in Love

Dating

Any woman who has been in a serious relationship for a reasonable length of time will don her best pair of rose-tinted glasses when contemplating the long-ago days when she first started dating her beloved. She will sigh with yearning and nostalgia as she recalls those blissful days when he didn't trim his toenails with his teeth/ fart in bed and hold her head under the duvet/ fall asleep on the sofa and snore loudly throughout *EastEnders*/ refer to her mother as 'that bitch from hell'/ flirt with anything in a skirt/ pick his nose and wipe it on the arm of the sofa, and so on and so forth, *ad nauseam*.

But were things really so great back in the good old days? Are we, perhaps, just kidding ourselves that everything used to be peachy and perfect and cosy and romantic, in order to avoid the horrible truth that all the warning signs were there from the word go – warning signs that were accompanied by frantically flashing lights and deafening alarm bells? We must be. Ask a handful of your girlfriends to share some of their dating stories with you and you will be inundated with tales of such unimaginable horror that they would make Stephen King green with envy. And what is really terrifying is how many of these women ended up with the person they were describing. Although in some cases they made lucky escapes and dumped the man in question as soon as humanly possible, with good reason as you will see.

In any case, the reasons for sharing some of their stories with you are threefold: a) in order that we may finally see the light, throw away the rose-tinted specs and accept responsibility for our plight; b) to allow us to take comfort in the fact that however irritated we may get with our menfolk, however badly they may sometimes behave, there is always someone worse off than we are; and c) for sheer entertainment value, these stories can't be beaten.

〜〜〜〜〜〜〜〜〜〜〜〜〜〜〜

'When my best friend offered to set me up with
a guy she works with, I was hesitant at first, but
eventually decided to go for it as I trust her
judgement. I met Jim at a bar near my office,
figuring that I could always make a quick escape
after a drink or two if things weren't going well.
I was very pleasantly surprised, however: Jim was
funny, courteous, educated and nice-looking and we
were getting along swimmingly. Two drinks turned
into three or four and we ordered some food.

Later on in the evening, we decided to head off
to another bar, where there was a live band and
dancing. That's when I realised that Jim was
without doubt the worst dancer I had ever come
across. Oh my God, it was horrific. For a long time
he stood completely still on the dance-floor, not
moving a muscle, as if he were turned to stone,
then his whole body started vibrating violently
and his arms started flailing around. I thought he
was having an epileptic fit. People were actually
stood around staring in horror and shooting me
sympathetic looks as I awkwardly jigged about in
front of him. I was so embarrassed. It was so off-
putting that I decided then and there not to see him

again, despite his many nice qualities. Thankfully, I later realised how silly this was and we've been together for nearly two years. He's not allowed to dance in public now. I keep a tight rein on him.'

'My ex-boyfriend turned up to pick me up for our first date wearing what I can only describe as rags – torn jeans, a rather grubby t-shirt, trainers with biro scribblings all over them. He obviously hadn't bothered to shower or shave either. He looked as if he'd been sleeping rough under Waterloo Bridge. I immediately felt wildly overdressed. This was a big hint that the romantic candlelit dinner in an upmarket restaurant I had been hoping for wasn't on the cards, but nothing could have prepared me for the shock I felt when he pulled in to a McDonald's parking lot.

Yes, he took me to McDonald's on a date! It would have been understandable had we been teenagers or students, but we were both in our mid-twenties and he worked in advertising! So there I was, in my little black dress and heels, sitting in one of those horrible plastic booths, munching on a Big Mac and trying to pretend nothing was wrong.

At least he paid for the 'meal', though, which is not something he ever did on any of our subsequent dates. The fact that there were any subsequent dates at all is something that I will never forgive myself for.'

'My husband has the loudest, most annoying laugh. It starts off with a few strange wheezy noises, as if he's about to have an asthma attack, then it gradually builds up to a crescendo of noises that sound like someone is doing unspeakable things to a donkey – HeehawheehawHEEHAWHEEHAW! He throws his whole body into the laugh too. He doubles over, his shoulders shake, he slaps his fists down on his thighs, the works. It's quite something to behold.

On our first date, he took me to quite a posh restaurant and I was mortified when I first heard him laugh. I actually flinched violently, almost propelling myself out of my chair. People were staring and I could see a couple of the waiters sniggering. It was embarrassing, but I got over it pretty quickly because he was such a nice guy. His laugh still irritates me sometimes, but mostly I enjoy the startled looks we get from passers-by when he breaks out in public.'

'I had been dating Greg for a few weeks and things were going well. He was a bit dull, but nice enough and having been dumped by my last boyfriend in a particularly brutal way, I was glad to have some male attention. I was pleased, therefore, when he invited me to dinner at his house. I hadn't been there before and wanted to check out his place. He was pretty well off and had a high-flying job, so I was expecting a real bachelor pad – lots of leather sofas, plasma-screen TVs, modern art on the walls, that sort of thing.

Imagine my surprise then, when I walked into a lounge that looked like the set of a 70s sitcom. There was chintz everywhere and, horror of horrors, doilies on every available surface. Alarm bells started to ring at this point. We were sitting on the couch chatting, when in shuffled this incredibly sour-looking old woman. "Meet Mummy," he proudly said. "Mummy" looked at me as if I were something she'd scraped off the bottom of her shoe and completely ignored my outstretched hand. "Nice to meet you," I said. "That's a lie," she muttered. She was perceptive.

'It dawned on me then that this high-flying, forty-something executive still lived with his mother. It was all I could do to stop myself from running screaming from the house then and there. As it was, I forced myself to sit through dinner, which of course "Mummy" joined us for, trying to ignore the death-stares she was shooting at me. He kept checking that she was OK and leaping up to fetch things for her. I tried to be charitable, telling myself how nice it was that he cared for his elderly mother, but really it was nauseating, if not downright disturbing. After dinner, I made my excuses and left. I saw Greg a few times after that, but it was hard to get over the whole Norman Bates thing, so I broke it off soon after.'

Commitment phobes

The awful thing about a man who can't commit is that it is very easy to fall in love with him. At the beginning of the relationship he lavishes you with attention. He constantly tells you how beautiful you are; he buys you expensive gifts for no reason; he is reluctant to let you out of his sight and when you are not together he rings you up at three in the morning to tell you how much he misses you. Eventually you smugly start to believe that finally, for once in your life, you have met a man who is more into you than you are into him. His unconditional worship makes you think that you must be the living incarnation of the goddess Aphrodite. Before too long you are mentally planning your wedding and writing lists of your favourite baby names. And that's when it all starts to go horribly wrong.

For the merest hint that you are starting to think about a long-term future together is enough to send him into an uncontrollable panic. It doesn't have to be anything major; he doesn't need to find your secret baby-name list. It can be something as insignificant as leaving a toothbrush and a few spare pairs of knickers at his place. He'll wander into his loo one day and stop, bewildered, in the doorway for a minute or two. 'Something's wrong,' he'll think. 'What is it?' And then he spots it, that innocuous little toothbrush, sitting next to his on the bathroom counter. Only when he sees it, he doesn't see a toothbrush. Oh no. He sees a terrifying abyss looming before him. He sees a lifetime of marriage and kids and household chores and not being able to do exactly what he wants whenever he wants. And so off he runs, belting down the street as fast as his legs will carry him, occasionally glancing over his shoulder to make sure you are not in hot pursuit. Another one bites the dust.

We've all been there, and it's all rather depressing, isn't it? What usually happens when we are unfortunate enough to encounter one of these specimens is that we turn to vodka and chick flicks to cheer ourselves up. So let's do the same thing now and take a light-hearted look at some famous fictional commitment phobes that we love to hate or hate to love. (You'll have to provide your own vodka though.)

James Bond – Various

James, James, James. What are you like? You've had more women than the entire human race has had hot dinners. In fact, the only woman you haven't had your wicked way with is poor, plain Miss Moneypenny who is clearly pining away for you. Don't you think it's time you settled down? Do you want to end up a pathetic old lech, hanging around casinos, clutching martinis in your gnarly, arthritic hands, leering at girls young enough to be your granddaughters and trying to persuade them that you were once a dashing Don Juan in Her Majesty's Secret Service? Why don't you just pick one of your legions of lady friends and make a commitment before it's too late? Oh, but wait. You can't, can you? Because whenever things start to get serious, they end up being killed in some gruesome and fantastical way. Hmm, how convenient for you…

Rick Blaine – Casablanca

Cynical, disillusioned and self-centred Rick Blaine is a commitment phobe par excellence. Near the beginning of the film, he casually dumps his poor French girlfriend in a breathtakingly heartless manner.

'Where were you last night?' she whines.

'That's so long ago, I don't remember,' he smirks.

'Will I see you tonight?' she persists

'I never make plans that far ahead,' he replies. The bastard.

At this point, movie buff commitment phobes were already frantically taking notes, but they hadn't seen anything yet. Enter ex-lover Ilsa. After some lengthy shenanigans involving Nazis, spies and letters of transit, which are of no interest to the note-taking commitment phobes, Ilsa tells Rick that she still loves him and he seems quite pleased about this. He leads her to believe that he will help her husband escape the country while she remains behind with him. Only when the time comes, of course, he gets cold feet and delivers one of the most irritating and patronising brush-offs in cinema history. 'Ilsa, I'm no good at being noble, but it doesn't take much to see that the problems of three little people don't amount to a hill of beans in this crazy world. Someday you'll understand that. Here's looking at you, kid.' And with that, he practically throws her on to a plane and wonders off arm in arm with his policeman pal. Nice.

Daniel Cleaver – Bridget Jones's Diary

It's hard not to love Daniel Cleaver, with his floppy hair, sexy posh accent and love of big knickers, but the man is a bounder. A bounder and a cad. Which of course makes him even more attractive to singleton Bridget. Daniel shows all the classic signs of early-relationship commitment-phobe behaviour, bombarding Bridget with saucy emails and whisking her off on a romantic mini-break. Things soon take a turn for the worse, and Daniel, who breaks into a cold sweat at the mere mention of the word 'relationship', starts to show his true colours. 'So where's this chap of yours?' asks Bridget's pervy 'Uncle' Geoffrey. 'Working, eh? A likely tale! Off they run! Whee!' And indeed off he does run, with a skeletal American lawyer, thus propelling Bridget into the arms of Mark Darcy, who is dishy enough in his own way, but let's face it, also a wee bit dull, despite valiant efforts to make himself more interesting by swearing and indulging in a spot of street brawling. You're not really fooling anyone, Mark.

John Willoughby – Sense and Sensibility

Who can forget the scene where Willoughby appears on the grey, windswept horizon on his trusty steed and rescues Marianne Dashwood, who has fallen and twisted her ankle, as girls of that era were wont to do (why didn't they invest in some sensible shoes if they were going to be running around the countryside in the pouring rain?). He scoops Marianne up as if she is light as a feather (no mean feat considering this was before Kate Winslet decided to join the ranks of all the other slimline Hollywood actresses) and thus seals the deal. Marianne falls head over heels in love with her knight in shining armour. But the knight in shining armour turns out to be a knight in not-very-shining armour. Indeed, you'd be hard pressed to find armour more rusty, tarnished and shoddily made. After much flirting and wooing, Willoughby cruelly rejects Marianne, coldly calling her 'Madam' when he bumps into her at a party, and ends up marrying some stuck-up rich bird, which I suppose is a commitment of sorts, albeit to wodges of cash. Poor Marianne nearly dies 'of a broken heart' (in reality a nasty bout of flu caused by yet more running around in the pouring rain) and, in her weakened state, is persuaded into a life of terminal boredom with the nice but deadly dull Colonel Brandon. Perhaps he and Mark Darcy should compare notes.

Danny Zucco – Grease

'Men are rats. They're fleas on rats. Worse than that, they're amoebas on fleas on rats,' says the wonderful, pink-haired Frenchy. A bit harsh as a general statement, maybe, but it certainly does apply to the loathsome Danny Zucco. Perhaps we should give him a break, as he is, after all, a teenager and teenagers aren't really big on commitment. Although, confusingly, the entire student population of Rydell High look to be well into their thirties. Indeed, some of them look older than the teachers. Funny sort of school. Anyhow, should we give Danny a break due to his supposed youth? No, let's not. Because he really is horrid.

Danny and Sandy hook up on holiday and have a lovely time innocently holding hands and gambolling around on sun-drenched beaches. How sweet. At the end of the holiday Danny waves Sandy off as she returns to her native Australia, no doubt breathing a huge sigh of relief. Then, to his barely disguised horror, she unexpectedly rolls up at Rydell High, expecting them to pick up where they left off. Danny reluctantly agrees and things go more or less smoothly for a while, until he tries to persuade her to have sex with him in the back of his car in full view of hundreds of other horny teenagers at a drive-in cinema. When she refuses, he storms off in a sulk. Cue much mournful singing.

After some on again, off again foolishness and a lot more singing, Sandy decides to take matters into her own hands. How does she do this? She turns up at the end-of-term party dressed in a skin-tight leather catsuit, an outfit that even the lowliest street hooker would think twice about wearing. Now that his ex looks like an absolute tart, Danny of course realises that perhaps he does love her after all and they go off into the sunset in, of all things, a flying car, to live happily ever after. Or at least until the next scantily clad blonde catches his wandering eye. Poor, deluded Sandy.

Arguments

While studying the way of life of native people in a remote village in Papua New Guinea, anthropologist Deborah Cameron witnessed one hell of a row between a husband and wife, which began when the wife fell through a hole in the floor of their home. Furious at her husband's poor workmanship, she placed the blame squarely on him. He in turn resented his manhood being called into question and hit her with a piece of sugar cane, whereupon all hell broke loose and she broke into a *kros*, a traditional angry tirade which is delivered at top volume in order to broadcast the victim's crimes to the entire village and which can last for nearly an hour.

'You are a f****** rubbish man!' she screamed. 'Your p**** is full of maggots! Stone balls! You have built me a house that I just fall down in and you hit me on the arm with a piece of sugar cane! You f****** mother's ****!' And so on in the same vein. Throughout all this, the man remained utterly silent, as is the local custom.

Other than the woman's impressive and admirable grasp of the fine art of insult-slinging (you've got to love 'stone balls'), two things strike one about this scenario: 1) shoddy DIY skills are not limited to Western men who have watched one too many episodes of *DIY SOS* (see DIY), and 2) when hit by the full force of a woman's wrath men the world over tend to retreat into silence.

This, as most women will agree, is not satisfactory. There is nothing worse, when you have built up a stomach-churning mix of self-pity and righteous indignation which needs to be given the only possible outlet – that of a jolly good barney – before your head explodes, than being confronted by an impenetrable stony silence. It's like repeatedly running at and throwing yourself against a brick wall, until all the bones in your body are broken and you are lying on the floor in a crumpled heap, a shattered shell of your former self.

Men think they are somehow diffusing the situation by completely ignoring their ranting womenfolk, but what they are doing is totally invalidating our feelings. They are saying, 'Lady, you are crazy. I have no idea what you are harping on about and I don't wish to be enlightened. Please leave me alone so I can snooze on the sofa in peace.' This only serves to ensure that the situation spirals out of all control. Imagine, if you will, such tactics being used during complicated international peace talks.

∞ ∞ ∞ ∞ ∞ ∞ ∞ ∞ ∞ ∞ ∞ ∞ ∞ ∞

Delegate A: If I could just have a moment to air some of our more serious grievances. We feel that these sanctions are grossly unfair and we would like you to explain why you feel they are necessary.

Delegate B: …[Smirks. Picks nose and examines the contents closely]

Delegate A: It's just that if you could give us some reasons we might be able to reach some kind of satisfactory compromise.

Delegate B: …[Rolls eyes, looks at watch]

Delegate A: You're really starting to annoy me now. What's your problem? Can't we discuss the situation like reasonable adults?

Delegate B: …[Sighs heavily. Picks up copy of *FHM* and starts reading article about Lindsay Lohan's boob jobs.]

Delegate A: You hate us, don't you? You don't care about our feelings at all. You wish you'd never entered into negotiations with our country. You wish you'd gone off with that other country that had its eye on you, the younger, richer one. You INSENSITIVE PIG!

Delegate B: … [Makes swirly 'you are mental' gesture and starts fiddling with mobile phone]

Delegate A: Right, that's it! No more Mr Nice Delegate! We'll show you! You'll be sorry! [Runs out of conference room, wild sobbing heard in corridor]

So you see, the equation here is simple: Grievances to air + silence = escalating situation + all-out war. This is no way to resolve conflict.

∽∾ ∽∾ ∽∾ ∽∾ ∽∾ ∽∾ ∽∾ ∽∾ ∽∾ ∽∾

Communication

It is a common misconception that men are straight-forward when it comes to expressing themselves. Men love to gather together in sad little groups down the pub and whinge and moan about how their women never say what they mean or mean what they say, while at the same time smugly congratulating themselves on their honesty and lack of calculation when it comes to communicating with the opposite sex.

'Poor us!' they wail. 'We are so confused! They say "yes" when they mean "no", and "no" when they mean "maybe" and half the time we just don't know what the hell they are going on about. They do it on purpose, just to make our lives difficult. Those heartless wenches! If only we could do without them altogether, but we're desperate for a shag so we have to put up with it. If only they could be more like us and just say it like it is.'

They have worked so hard, bless them, to perpetuate this myth that we women have reached a point where we almost believe it is true, and they are absolutely convinced that it is. But of course it isn't. Not by a long shot.

⌒⌒⌒⌒⌒⌒⌒⌒⌒⌒⌒⌒⌒⌒⌒⌒⌒

What he says and what he really means

He says: Where is the newspaper/spare key/golf bag/remote control?
He means: I know exactly where it is; it's where it always is. I'm just lazy and am hoping that by feigning confusion you'll fetch it for me.

He says: We're not lost. I know exactly where we are.
He means: We're hopelessly lost. I'm terrified that eventually you'll realise that we've been driving round in circles for the last hour and you'll bang on all night about how I should have asked for directions. I should have asked for directions, shouldn't I?

He says: It's a guy thing. You wouldn't understand.
He means: It defies all logic and reason and I have no idea how to explain it to you without sounding like an utter berk.

He says: I bought you these flowers on the way home just to let you know that I love and appreciate you.

He means: I've done something very stupid. I hope you never find out, but just in case you do, here are some hastily bought flowers that I can use as ammunition when the inevitable argument wanders into 'you never do anything nice for me' territory.

He says: I don't know what I want.
He means: I don't know what I want, but I'm pretty sure I don't want you.

He says: Of course I don't mind if you go out with the girls tonight. I'll be a bit lonely and I'll miss you, but don't worry about me. I'm sure I'll find something to keep me occupied.

He means: Woo! I get to spend the evening drinking way too many beers and watching endless repeats of *Top Gear* in peace. But I'm going to lay this little guilt-trip on you so that next time I want to go on an all-night bender with my mates, you won't be able to complain.

He says: I've got my reasons.
He means: I'm desperately trying to think of one good reason for doing what I did.

He says: That dinner you cooked tonight was delicious and you look beautiful in that new top.
He means: I'm hoping to get some tonight.

He says: I love you so much.
He means: I'm really, really hoping to get some tonight.

He says: Your friend, X, she's nice, isn't she?
He means: Your friend is hot! I really fancy her.

He says: I can't believe your friend Y is still single. I think we should set her up with someone.
He means: I hate the fact that your friend is still

single. Every time you go out with her, I spend the evening torturing myself imagining you both out on the town, pulling everything in sight. I think we should set her up with someone, no matter how unsuitable, so that she is no longer an imaginary threat to our relationship.

He says: Of course I've been listening to you!
He means: Uh oh. I stopped listening to you half an hour ago and have been surreptitiously watching *Coronation Street* over your shoulder. I hope you don't ask me to repeat what you were saying …
Oh God, you just have. I'm in big trouble now.

He says: That outfit looks amazing on you! That's definitely the one.
He means: Good grief, woman! How many outfits are you going to try on before you make a decision! I've got to get you out of the door right now or we'll turn up at the dinner party four days late.

He says: I missed you.
He means: Never, never go away for a break without me again, I beg you. The house is in utter chaos, I can't find the kids, the cat's moved in with

the next-door neighbour, there's no food in the fridge and I've been sitting here in my grubby dressing gown for three days now because I don't know how the washing machine works and I have no clean clothes to wear.

Lotharios

An attractive woman sits alone in a crowded, noisy bar. She is reading a newspaper and sipping a drink and occasionally glances at her watch. She is clearly waiting for someone. Nearby, a group of red-faced, middle-aged men in suits are getting stuck into their third or fourth round of drinks. They have been getting steadily louder and more raucous. Once in a while, one of them will glance over to check out the woman, then turn back and make a comment to his pals, whereupon they will guffaw with drunken laughter. The woman is making heroic efforts to ignore them. Eventually, to her horror, one of them gets up. 'Oh no. Please no. Don't come over here,' she thinks to herself. 'Perhaps he's just going to the loo.' But no, the group falls silent as their intrepid friend swaggers his way across to the woman's table. The woman visibly braces herself.

'Did it hurt?' the man asks.

'I'm sorry?'

'Did it hurt?' he repeats, slightly louder this time. She can hear his friends sniggering.

'Did what hurt?'

'When you fell from heaven.'

There is a long, embarrassed pause.

'Look, I don't mean to be rude, but I'm waiting for a friend and...'

The man interrupts. 'Oh come on, darling. Don't be like that. Come and have a drink with us.'

'Thanks, but I'm really not interested.'

'Suit yourself. You don't know what you're missing.'

The man weaves his way back to his table, shrugging his shoulders and grinning inanely. His pals chortle and guffaw once more and the woman distinctly hears the phrases 'Must be a lesbian' and 'Not that good-looking anyway.'

Sadly, this is a scenario that is played out in every bar across the country, every day of the week.

Flirting is good. It is an essential human interaction, and without it nobody would ever get together with anyone and the human race would die out. Men and women have been making eyes at each other over the campfire and asking, 'Your cave or mine?' since time immemorial. But why, in this day and age, when we are bombarded with flirting techniques from every magazine, newspaper and television channel, when there are entire books devoted to the art of the pick-up, must woman still have to put up with these ham-fisted, embarrassingly inappropriate attempts at seduction? A little finesse, gentlemen, please. It's not rocket science.

∾ ∾ ∾ ∾ ∾ ∾ ∾ ∾ ∾ ∾ ∾ ∾

1. When you speak to us, look us in the eye. If you really fancy us, a glance at our mouths every now and then works wonders. But, please, keep your eyes above our necks. We love our breasts too. They are womanly and attractive and biologically very handy. They are indeed wondrous things. But they have not yet mastered the art of conversation; they won't reply to you, no matter how persistent you are.

2. If you are married, please do not approach us in bars or nightclubs or wherever it is you may be. You probably shouldn't be there at all. Go home to your wife and don't forget to buy her a big bunch of flowers on the way. If you really insist

on trying to wow us with your pathetic attempts at seduction, at least have the brains to take your wedding ring off first.

3. Whistling is for dogs and Captain von Trapp's children. Not for us. Are we dogs? No, actually, don't answer that – categorically, we are not. What do you think is going to happen when you whistle piercingly at a woman in the street? Do you think she will march over, smile seductively and say, 'Well, hello to you too, handsome. What are you doing tonight?' If one day the impossible should happen and a woman actually responded in such a manner, you would probably fall off your scaffolding in shock. And that would be a good thing.

୧୨ ୧୨ ୧୨ ୧୨ ୧୨ ୧୨ ୧୨ ୧୨ ୧୨ ୧୨ ୧୨

And for the ladies, a timely, well-delivered, none-too-subtle slap-down is often the only way to ensure your would-be suitors get the message loud and clear.

He says: If I could see you naked, I'd die happy.
You reply: If I could see you naked, I'd die laughing.

He says: If I could rearrange the alphabet, I'd put I and U together.
You reply: Well, if I could rearrange the alphabet, I'd put F and U together.

He says: Haven't I seen you someplace before?
You reply: Yeah, that's why I don't go there anymore.

He says: So, wanna go back to my place?
You reply: Well, I don't know. Will two people fit under a rock?

He says: Is this seat empty?
You reply: Yes, and this one will be too if you sit down.

He says: I'd like to call you. What's your number?
You reply: It's in the phone book.
But he persists: But I don't know your name.
Deliver the final blow: That's in the phone book too.

Present buying

When it comes to the subtle art of gift-giving many men are stumped. Even the most thoughtful chap can panic when faced with the prospect of having to carefully tip-toe through the minefield that is choosing an appropriate present for the woman he loves. We've all been in the position of receiving a gift we absolutely hate from a loved one, and it is not a pleasant experience. There you sit, heart hammering in anticipation as you eye the package your dearly beloved is clutching in his sweaty little paws. 'What is it?' you think. 'Could it be that one of the numerous hints I've been dropping daily for the last six months has sunk in and he's actually bought me those Jimmy Choos I've been lusting after for so long? The box looks the right size....' Unable to contain your excitement, you grab the present, rip off the wrapping paper and open the box to reveal... a new iron. 'An iron?!' you think to yourself (because by this point you will be beyond the capacity for coherent speech), 'AN IRON!?' And then you will either burst into tears or throw the offending item at his head with the kind of force that only a furious and disappointed woman can muster, depending on your temperament.

So what are the worst offenders, the gifts no woman in her right mind would wish to see in her Christmas stocking, the offerings that make us want to throttle our menfolk with our bare hands?

Exercise equipment

'Dear Thunder Thighs, wishing you a very happy birthday, with love from your soon-to-be-ex-husband,' says the accompanying card. Well, it probably doesn't, but it may as well. In much the same vein, being given diet books, lifelong WeightWatchers memberships and – horror of horrors – fat-free chocolates is also grounds for a bitter, acrimonious break-up.

Stuffed animals

Are you twelve years old? Or one of those women who dress only in pink, excel at baby talk and still play with their Barbies? If not, you probably have no use for a two-foot-tall stuffed bear clutching a satin heart with 'I wuv you' written on it in swirly writing.

Household gadgets

Anything designed to make housework easier is not a suitable gift. A necessity, yes; a token of undying love and devotion, no. Just because he goes into paroxysms of orgasmic delight whenever he opens a box containing yet another useless power tool doesn't mean you will feel the same way about a new vacuum cleaner or mop, no matter how high-tech or expensive.

Stuff he wants

This is the oldest trick in the book, so transparent that a two-year-old child would see right through it, and yet still they do it. He'll sit there grinning while you, a woman in her thirties, pull a PlayStation 3 out of its packaging. Then he'll settle happily down to an afternoon of shooting things with big guns, while you retire to the kitchen to shed a few bitter tears.

Flowers

Gentlemen, it pains me to burst this particular bubble, but it must be done. A bunch of flowers, unaccompanied by any other gift, just will not cut it when it comes to the more important occasions that mark a lady's life, such as anniversaries and birthdays. Flowers are for days when you just want to show your wife or girlfriend how much you appreciate her or for when you have misbehaved in some way. On a day of celebration, a little more thought is required. It wouldn't be so bad if you bought a big, beautiful bunch of expensive roses, but you rarely do. It's usually a tiny, sorry-looking bouquet of half-dead blooms in hideously clashing colours snatched from a garage forecourt in a last-minute panic. Nothing says, 'I'm sorry. I forgot' more clearly.

Novelty items

Musical socks, wind-up action figures that make obscene gestures, anything with the word 'fart' on the packaging. These things are suitable only for office Secret Santas and whacky Uncle Bill who collects whoopee cushions and likes to do Tommy Cooper impressions.

'Sexy' lingerie

Many women would be overjoyed to receive a frivolous wisp of silk and lace from some upmarket boutique, but the purchase of truly desirable lingerie is too fraught with perils for the average man to pull off with aplomb. For a start, their idea of what is sexy is rarely the same as ours. Crotchless panties and cut-out bras may seem to them to be the zenith of erotic sophistication; we can only cringe at their impracticability and tackiness. And then there is the size issue. Either the item in question is ludicrously small, thus casting the recipient into the deepest of self-loathing glooms, or miles too big (a 36 GG bra), which equally leads to feelings of inadequacy. A minefield indeed – and one best avoided at all costs.

Cheap knock-offs

The problem with stuff that 'fell off the back of a lorry' is that it generally looks like it has literally fallen off (or been hurled from) the back of a lorry. Crushed packaging, misspelled logos (there's no 'h' in Gucci) and shoddy stitching are all easy-to-spot clues that our men have been scrimping on the present front. It's not that we expect them to splurge their life savings on a Luis Vuitton handbag, it's just that we would rather have a decently made high-street version than one that has been knocked together out of nasty shiny plastic by some unfortunate children in a sweatshop in China.

Uniquely Male

Sensory deficiencies

There is a mild neurological condition known as Sensory Deficiency Disorder where the brain has difficulty processing information from the five senses and which, according to that fount of all knowledge Wikipedia, 'may cause distress and confusion'. Of course a condition like this is nothing to laugh about and not for a moment would we suggest that all men suffer from it, but there are certain parallels that can be drawn between this and the fact that many men are seemingly able to see and hear only what they want to see and hear. It is an extraordinary and enviable gift, but it can certainly lead to much distress and confusion.

Impaired vision

The first sign that a man's sight is not all it should be is the 'Where is the…?' syndrome. 'Where is the remote control?' he whines. You can see it, of course. It's sitting on the coffee table where it always is, mere inches away from him, plain as day. But, for your own amusement, you decide to say nothing. He half-heartedly digs around under the sofa cushions for a couple of seconds, but without actually getting up from his semi-reclined position. 'I can't find it and the Grand Prix is about to start.' He looks at you with sad, puppy-dog eyes, nearly in tears at the prospect of missing a few minutes of watching cars go round and round in circles at top speed. You shrug and go back to reading your magazine. He sighs heavily and starts looking wildly around the room, peering into corners and up at the ceiling, as if he is expecting to see the remote control dangling from the light fitting, but he still doesn't get up from his comfy seat. The tension is building and he is very distressed now. It is at this point that the 'Where is the…?' form of questioning morphs into its more aggressive version, namely the 'What have you done with the…?' interrogation technique. 'But what have you done with it?' he demands. You're tempted to tell him that you've fed it to the dog or released it into the wild,

but you've had enough now.
'I haven't done anything
with it! It's RIGHT IN
FRONT OF YOU!' He
looks shocked at
your outburst, which
annoys you even more.
'All right! There's no need to
be like that! I was just asking…'

Another, equally exasperating form of this condition is
the 'Do we have any…?' syndrome. 'Do we have any…?'
actually translates as 'Fetch me the…'. 'Do we have any
butter?' he asks as you sit down to have your dinner. He
knows there is butter. There's always butter because all
hell breaks loose if he is not able to slather mounds of
artery-hardening saturated fat on his bread. Every time
he opens the fridge it is there, right in front of his eyes.
But his brain refuses to accept the signal being sent to it
by his eyes because it knows that if it acknowledges
the exact positioning of the butter dish, it will have to
direct its master's body to perform several complex
manoeuvres in order to go and fetch the butter – bend
knees, push back chair, get up from chair, one foot in
front of the other all the way to the fridge. And this is just
way too much effort.

Impaired hearing

He watches TV with the sound turned up so high that the walls shake and the family next door are all on Valium for their shattered nerves. He wires his music system up to speakers so enormous that there is no room in the lounge for any other furniture and getting to the kitchen is like undertaking a gruelling army-training obstacle course. He and his mates yell at each other across tiny, cramped pub tables. When he rings you, he shouts so loudly that you can put the phone down and carry on with what you were doing in the next room and still be able to hear him.

You'd be forgiven for thinking, therefore, that it is this penchant for living life at top decibel that has caused him to be seemingly all but deaf. This is not the case, however. His ability to hear is entirely selective; he can switch it on and off at will.

'I'm fed up with you today,' you might say to him. 'You promised me you were going to help me tidy up. All you've done this afternoon is sit around watching football. If you don't switch it off and put some of the clean laundry away, I'll pour all your beer down the sink and you won't be getting any sex for the next week.'

What he actually hears is this: 'Blah, blah, blah, blah, football, blah, blah, blah, blah, beer, blah, blah, blah, blah, sex, blah, blah.'

And then there are scenarios like this one. You get home from the supermarket, open the front door and call out to him. 'Could you help me unload the car?' There's no reply, but you're sure he heard you. He's only in the front room, a few feet away, and for once the TV is switched off and there is no loud music rattling the foundations of the house. You go back to the car. A few moments pass. Where is he? Back you go to the door. 'I need help unloading the car!' You raise your voice this time.

'What?!' he shouts back.

'HELP ME UNLOAD THE CAR!' He must have heard you this time. Everyone on the entire street must have heard you this time. But there is still no sign of him. You struggle inside with the bags, red-faced and furious, and pop your head round the living-room door.

'Thanks so much for the help. I really appreciate it.' Your voice is dripping with sarcasm.

'I couldn't hear what you were saying!' he says, a look of outraged innocence on his face.

You stomp off to the kitchen and put the kettle on. 'Do you want a cup of tea?' you ask, in the merest hint of a barely-there whisper. 'Yes, please. Two sugars. Thanks!' is the instant reply.

Men and their mothers

My mother-in-law dropped by today. I knew it
was her because when she knocked on the door,
the mice threw themselves into the traps.

What does a mother-in-law call her broom?
Basic transportation.

Two cannibals were sitting down to lunch.
One says to the other, 'You know, I really can't
stand my mother-in-law.' The other replies, 'Well,
put her to the side and just eat the mashed
potatoes.'

Did you know that if you rearrange the letters
in 'mother-in-law' you get 'woman Hitler'?

What is the definition of 'mixed feelings'? Seeing
your mother-in-law drive off a cliff in your new
Mercedes.

Mother-in-law jokes are as old as the hills. They have been around since the very first mother-in-law sauntered uninvited into her beloved offspring's cave, running her fingers along the walls to check for dust and peering suspiciously into the cooking pot to make sure her darling boy was being adequately fed, all the time casting death stares at his poor, long-suffering spouse, tutting under her breath and generally making a nuisance of herself.

Of course, not all mother-in-laws are broom-riding, cauldron-stirring old witches. There are many wonderful mothers who take a healthy interest in their sons' lives, delighting in their triumphs and commiserating with them when things don't go according to plan, while managing not to interfere too much. But there is a certain type of woman who looks at her offspring and does not see a grown man with a job, a mortgage, credit cards, a family of his own and a rapidly receding hairline. No, she still sees the small boy he used to be, with short trousers, grazes on his knees and a runny nose. He is still a helpless little creature that cannot survive in the big bad world without help from his mummy.

A recent survey found that one in three men between the ages of 20 and 35 is still living at home, compared to just one in six women of the same age. That's *one-third* of men in this age bracket. This seems like quite an astonishing figure until you stop to think about it. Because why would they want to move out and face the real world like the big boys they are? Their clothes are washed and ironed, their beds are made, their meals are cooked for them, their packed lunches are ready on the counter for them to take to work every morning, and all this for very little in return. These KIPPERS (Kids in Parents' Pockets Eroding Retirement Savings) know they've got a good thing going on.

The unconditional love that a mother has for her children is a wonderful thing, but when this love strays into the disturbing arena of 'smother love' then the consequences can be hugely damaging. Because what happens when one of these overgrown Peter Pans finally decides to grow himself a backbone and learn to stand on his own two feet? He finds that he can't.

He may move out of the parental home. He may even find some unfortunate woman willing to put up with him. But he will always love mother best. Nothing the new woman in his life does can ever match up to mummy's exacting standards. His underpants are not ironed. His towel is not put into the tumble dryer while he is in the shower so that it is all warm and snuggly when he emerges. He is expected to blow his own nose and wipe his own bottom without any prompting. His food is presented to him without any sort of smiley face made out of bits of tomato. Nobody calls him at work to remind him that the weather is turning and anxiously enquire as to whether he is wearing a vest. Oh, the horror of it all!

The umbilical cord was cut at birth, but it is still there in spirit, tying him to his mum for as long as they are both still alive. All you can do is hope and pray that the bond doesn't last beyond this, à la Norman Bates in *Psycho*.

Jokers

It seems to be a universally accepted fact that women can't tell jokes. Fair enough; there is much truth to this ('A rabbi and a priest were in a helicopter and…oh, wait, no, it was a speedboat. A rabbi and a priest were in a speedboat and…actually, no, I was right the first time. They were in a helicopter and there was this camel and the priest said, "Why the long face?" No, that can't be right, I'll start again…'). But the point that many men miss when they pour derision on women's apparent inability to remember what comes after 'Knock, knock' is that jokes (as opposed to witty one-liners or well-delivered amusing anecdotes) are very rarely funny. In fact, they are usually excruciatingly unfunny and should be confined to the playground or to cracker-joke sessions round the table after Christmas lunch, when everyone is so pissed that even the Queen's annual sombre speech is a cause for side-splitting hilarity.

Unfortunately, there is a certain type of man who cannot grasp this fact. We all know one of these specimens, a sadly common subspecies of man known as the Joker. The Joker delights in unleashing a torrent of corny or offensive jokes at the most inappropriate moments. You could be in the middle of a sophisticated little dinner party, enjoying a heated but nonetheless civilised conversation about politics or religion or the state of the economy and the Joker will chime in with, 'Have you heard the one about the bishop and the actress?' in the mistaken belief that he is somehow lightening the mood. Of course what he is really doing is ensuring that the mood takes a sudden nose-dive as everyone is forced to halt mid-conversation and listen to his inanities, rictus grins on faces, waiting for the pathetic punchline. Or you could be busy at work, frantically trying to meet a deadline, when you are distracted by the resident office Joker regaling a group of guffawing male co-workers with a non-stop stream of gags, usually involving some form of misogynistic or racial stereotypes. In which case, unless you want to be forever known as the office party-pooper, you are forced to grit your teeth, attempt to block him out and fantasise about marching over and slamming your flat-screen monitor down over his head. As Mark Twain once said, 'It's better to be silent and be thought a fool, than to speak and remove all doubt.'

The Joker rarely stops at just spewing out a few corny gags though. Oh no. Quite often he will also have a penchant for endlessly quoting lines from popular comedy classics. Who can forget Tony Blair's cringe-inducing 'Am I bovvered?' or Richard Madeley's painful Ali G impersonation ('Is it because I is black?' No, Richard, it is because you are a prat)?

Worse even than this, if such a thing is possible, is the Joker's love of items of novelty clothing. Guys, a tip for you: when women see you wearing these crimes against fashion we do not think, 'Oh wow, look at him! What a crazy, whacky, fun-loving dude! He must be a laugh a minute! He's the guy for me!' Please, we beg you, leave the Homer Simpson ties and musical socks to your uncle Bill to wear at Christmas to match his Rudolph the Red-Nosed Reindeer jumper.

By far the most dangerous and obnoxious type of Joker (a sub-subspecies, if you will), however, is the

Practical Joker. Granted, practical jokes can be highly amusing, given the right circumstances and a certain degree of sensitivity towards your intended victim, but the seasoned Practical Joker, of the type we are discussing here, is more often than not a law unto himself, a blot on civilised society. His side-splitting antics are carefully planned to cause maximum annoyance and embarrassment to their victims. Beware the Practical Joker: his finely honed mayhem-causing skills are awesome to behold. You cannot beat him at his own game. You have been warned.

∽∞∽∞∽∞∽∞∽∞∽∞∽∞∽∞

Practical jokers unmasked: the monsters lurking in our midst

'A rather unpopular colleague was out of the office on a business trip and was due back on Christmas Eve. Those of us unfortunate enough to have to work that day decided to surprise him with a festive gift, or rather gifts. There was plenty of wrapping paper about so we set to work wrapping up various items on his workstation. The initial plan was to just wrap up his monitor, keyboard, mouse and phone, but we got a bit carried away.

In the end we spent almost the whole day carefully wrapping up every single item on his desk and in his drawers. We even wrapped all his biros and pencils individually and we rolled up his paperwork into little tubes and wrapped them as well. We made sure to use plenty of sticky tape, to cause maximum inconvenience. His flight was delayed, so he showed up at the office just as we were all leaving for the Christmas break. The look on his face was priceless and we were all helpless with laughter. He had to write a report before he left, so he had no choice but to get straight to work undoing all our handiwork. Apparently it took the poor sucker hours and he didn't leave the office until close to midnight.'

'My brother and his girlfriend asked me to feed their cats while they were away for three weeks on holiday. I immediately spotted a golden opportunity for mischief-making and spent a good week or so trying to come up with something suitably annoying. One day, as I was sitting around in my brother's flat, drinking his beer with a mate, I had a stroke of genius. We decided to do a spot of interior decorating. We moved all the living room

furniture into their bedroom and vice-versa.
Then we rearranged all the kitchen cupboards and
drawers. My brother is tidy almost to the point of
being obsessive-compulsive, so you can imagine
his fury when he got home, exhausted and jet-
lagged, to find his home completely topsy-turvy.
He didn't speak to me for a month after that, but
it was worth it.'

'My sister has been terrified of clowns ever since
she was a kid. A few years ago, she slept on my
sofa for a few days while she was having some
work done to her house. One night, I set my
alarm for the early hours and spent half an hour
painting my face with clown make-up: deathly
white face, eerie red smile, red nose, the works.
I then crept into the pitch-dark living room,
crouched down next to her, shone a torch directly
into my face and shook her awake. Oh my God,
the screams. I've never heard anything like it.'

'My ex-boss was a real piece of work. I couldn't
stand him. Of all his rotten qualities, the worse was
that he always took credit for other people's work.
He used to make me put together a PowerPoint

presentation every week, which he would then present himself to the board of directors, passing it off as his own. Hours of work each week, with absolutely no acknowledgement. I finally got myself a better job and handed in my notice. I decided to sabotage the final presentation I had to prepare. I gathered together a collection of office party photos. Now, this guy was a real drunken lech, so there were plenty of pretty incriminating photographs of him. Instead of the usual boring pie charts and graphs, I put in pictures of him downing pints, leering at female colleagues and one particularly choice one of him passed out under a table in some bar. Nice. Unfortunately, I never attended these presentations, but a female colleague was taking the minutes and she said it worked beautifully. He didn't glance at the screen as he droned on and on, so the directors had a good long time to take in his drunken antics before he finally cottoned on. Ah, sweet revenge!'

Office offenders

Men tend to behave differently in the workplace than they do when they are with their nearest and dearest. After all, farting loudly then laughing hysterically or saying to the boss, 'Stop nagging! I'll finish the report when the footie's over' is generally considered to be poor business etiquette. This does not mean, however, that there isn't plenty of annoying male behaviour to be witnessed around the average office.

The Lech

The Lech simply cannot keep his hands out of his trouser pockets. They reside there all day long. There is much rummaging and jiggling, often accompanied by the clinking of coins. It's disgusting, but somehow it's impossible not to occasionally glance at the offending area, which of course pleases him and encourages yet more fiddling. It's a hellish vicious circle.

Any female co-worker is fair game to the Lech, be she 16 or 60. He'll perch one buttock on the edge of your desk and engage you in conversation when you are at your busiest, making sure that he throws in an inappropriate sexual innuendo every couple of seconds and all the time staring unblinkingly at your cleavage. He never fails to pass some creepy comment on your choice of outfit, as if he were some kind of fashion guru. If you ask him to take a look at something on your computer (don't ever do this), he will stand behind you as you sit at your desk, pressing himself against your chair, and you will be forced to lean further and further forwards until your face is squashed against your keyboard.

Mr Buzzword

'It's essential that we think outside the box when we're working on fast-tracking the synergised, client-focused new benchmark. Let's touch base on this game plan soon; I don't want you to be out of the loop.' What on earth is he talking about? Nobody seems to know; they just nod and smile politely as he blathers on. The fact of the matter is that he doesn't know what he is talking about either. He is deliberately avoiding using plain English in order to confuse you so much that you don't cotton on to the fact that he is crap at his job.

The Slacker

No matter how busy the office, no matter how many urgent deadlines need to be met, the Slacker somehow avoids doing any work whatsoever. His job is simply a minor annoyance that gets in the way of his busy social life. He spends hours making personal calls, playing solitaire and reorganising his Fantasy Football Team and yet he avoids getting the sack. How does he do this? Simple. Whenever the boss makes an appearance, he starts shuffling bits of paper around his desk or typing frantically. He is reviled by his fellow co-workers, but mostly because they are all secretly jealous of his astounding slacking skills.

Mr Decibel

He can't do anything quietly; everything is at top volume. He stomps around the office as if he has anvils attached to his feet. Rather than hauling his lazy bum out of his chair and going over to speak to a co-worker, he will shout across the entire office. Everybody knows every detail of what is going on in his personal and professional life because he yells at the top of his lungs whenever he makes a call, having seemingly failed to grasp the fact that the miracle of the telephone is that it allows one to speak directly into the listener's ear. Even when he's not on a call or screaming across the office, he's incapable of not making noise. Every time he picks up a piece of paper, he sighs; every time he reads an email, loud sighing; every time he stands up or sits down, more sighing, as if the world is coming to an end and all he can do is watch.

The Slob

Everyone avoids him for fear that they might catch something nasty. His idea of personal hygiene is to slap on copious amounts of cheap aftershave in a pathetic attempt to cover up the odour of BO and stale cigarette smoke. He coughs and splutters constantly without covering his mouth. He eats at his desk, making noises never before heard outside of a zoo – you didn't think it was possible for anyone to crunch soup, but somehow he manages it – and slurps at his lukewarm mug of tea as if it were molten lava. His desk looks like something that has crawled out from the pits of hell: crumbs everywhere, half-eaten mouldy sandwiches half buried under piles of coffee-stained paperwork and unidentifiable stains that you don't want to even think about.

Mr Competitive

No matter how accomplished you are, no matter how adventurous and exotic your hobbies, Mr Competitive has done it before. Not only that, he has done it bigger, better, faster and for longer. Did you go fishing at the weekend and catch a fifteen-pound trout? Well, Mr Competitive was ice-fishing at the North Pole and caught ten. Blindfolded. Whilst being fired at by a group of enraged Eskimos with machine guns.

The IT Geek

When your computer is on the blink, you want it fixed
right away. You do not want a three-hour monologue on
World of Warcraft, *Battlestar Galactica* or the outrageous
shenanigans that took place at last month's *Star Trek*
convention. Nor are you remotely interested in the
relative merits of Windows XP versus Windows Vista.
No, you do not collect comic books. Or action figures.
You just want the damn computer fixed.

So there you have it. Whether you've landed yourself a
lothario, a geek, a shed enthusiast, a cheapskate, a slob,
a mummy's boy, a nose-picker or some ungodly
combination of all of these, no doubt you will have
recognised within the pages of this book at least some of
the uniquely male foibles and peccadilloes that drive us
women mad on a regular basis.

And now that we've had a good old moan and a laugh
together, don't you feel a bit better? Don't you feel a bit
more equipped to deal with whatever new and interesting
way the man in your life has come up with to annoy the
hell out of you without resorting to physical violence and
a long stretch in the clink? Yes? Good. Job done, then.

Men, eh? Can't live with them, can't shoot them. But
we love them anyway. Most of the time.